CALGARY COOKS

GAIL NORTON / KAREN RALPH

FOREWORD BY JOHN GILCHRIST

CALGARY COOKS

Recipes from the City's Top Chefs

Figure 1

Vancouver / Berkeley

14 15 16 17 18 5 4 3 2 1

Cataloguing data available from Library and Archives Canada
ISBN 978-1-927958-08-7 (cloth)

Editing by Lucy Kenward
Copy editing by Iva Cheung
Cover and interior design by Naomi MacDougall
Cover photographs by John Sherlock and Maggie Lennon
Interior photographs by John Sherlock, except for images by Maggie Lennon on the following pages: 19, 38, 70, 76, 85, 93, 101, 116, 128, 133, 145, 149, 150, 155, 184 and the following numbered chef photos: 03, 08, 14, 18, 19, 20, 22, 24, 28, 29, 31, 32, 35, 36, 37, 38

Photographs taken at The Cookbook Co.
Printed and bound in China by C&C Offset Printing Co., Ltd.
Distributed in the U.S. by Publishers Group West

Figure 1 Publishing Inc.
Vancouver, BC Canada
www.figure1pub.com

Contents

Foreword

During my decades of reviewing restaurants, I've lusted after many a recipe. I might be sitting in the comfy western Mediterranean climes of Candela, wondering how chef Rogelio Herrera creates his unique watermelon and tuna ceviche. Or I might be immersed in the modernist black-and-white tones of MARKET, contemplating chef Dave Bohati's take on Portuguese pork and clams using pork belly and scallops. Or I might be entranced by the silky richness of chef Glen Manzer's linguine alla carbonara at Bonterra.

But how can I recreate this dish at home? I can read from the menu that Manzer's carbonara includes wild boar bacon, chilies, eggs and Grana Padano cheese. But how much? How is the sauce prepared? What comes first? At what temperature? And what about the pasta?

Sure, I can ask the chefs. And most of them will be more than happy to tell me. But they're cooking restaurant quantities using industrial equipment. And so much of the process is so natural to them that they often forget to include basic details. Like, use a pot. Or slice the onion. Let's not forget that some are Euro-trained, so they work in weights more than volumes. And many will say to "cook it until it looks done." What does that mean?

That's where this book comes in handy. Gail Norton and Karen Ralph have managed to wrangle forty of the top chefs in Calgary and extract recipes from them. They've translated those words into easy- (or at least easier-) to-use recipes for the home cook.

You may still have to stretch a bit. Your homecooked version of Roy Oh's *daeji bulgogi* may never taste quite as it does when he makes it at Anju, but that's part of the thrill. This book will help us come as close as possible to the flavours that the pros create.

So lust all you want. Now get cooking!

JOHN GILCHRIST
CBC Radio restaurant critic
Columnist for the *Calgary Herald* and *Avenue* Magazine
Author of *Cheap Eats*
October 2014

Introduction

Calgary in the 1980s was known for having many venues for live music, but the city's dining options were limited to steakhouses, Greek pizza parlours, Chinese food and hotel restaurants. Steak tartare, chopped and mixed tableside, or baron of beef served with a foil-wrapped baked potato topped with chives, sour cream and bacon bits and followed by pumpkin cheesecake seemed like the height of dining elegance. Pub grub was no better: it usually consisted of the classic beef-dip sandwich, pickled eggs and packets of chips.

Despite a stagnant food scene, Calgary's population was growing: people were arriving from across Canada and around the world for jobs in oil and gas. When the boom went bust, the newcomers stayed, creating the nucleus of what makes Calgary the interesting, culturally diverse city that it is today.

In 1982, we entered the "deli years" when Sam's on 4th Street opened. It was Calgary's original late-night deli, and it was an immediate success. The popular My Marvin's Deli, whose menus read, "You Don't Have to Be Jewish to Eat at My Marvin's," soon followed. We lined up around the block to eat Montreal smoked-meat sandwiches, Reubens filled with sauerkraut, cream cheese and lox on toasted bagels, and chopped liver on rye. At that time, one of the highlights of the week was going out to a café late at night to sip cappuccinos and eat decadent desserts. The caffeine and the sugar kept us awake all night, but it was a small price to pay for such a feeling of culture and sophistication.

Thanks to Alberta's large, well-established Eastern European population, we were familiar with perogies, cabbage rolls, dumplings, goulash, blintzes, blinis, latkes and kielbasa. These were the foods of our friends and families—foods that were staples at country fairs, fundraisers and bake sales. And we'd long had a thriving, vibrant Chinatown and could boast that George Wong of the Silver Inn here had invented ginger beef in 1974. However, Calgary's population kept growing, creating both the demand and market for more internationally diverse dining options. Our first taste of authentic Indian fare came in the early '80s, when a few new restaurants started offering such traditional dishes as samosas, pappadums and Madras curry while others reflected Britain's colonial influence with menus that featured these spicy flavours alongside bangers and mash and mushy peas.

It was clear that the food scene in Calgary was evolving when 4th Street Rose Restaurant and Bar offered a taste of casual, sunkissed California in the early 1980s, and we all fell in love with it. The space had large glass windows that gave it an atrium feel, exposed brick walls, terracotta floor tiles, an open kitchen, separate bar and charming, street-side patio. It was fresh, informal and exciting—and about as far from the dark, windowless, stuffy steakhouses and hotel dining rooms with their wallpaper and red carpets as one could get and still be in Calgary. We loved sitting at the bar, watching the action in the dining room, sipping margaritas from martini glasses and eating Caesar salads served in large flip-top glass jars.

When the stylish Mescalero and its downstairs bar, Crazy Horse, charged onto the scene in the late '80s, we went mad for its

Mexican and American Southwest–influenced décor, cuisine and cocktails. It was followed in 1989 by Cilantro Restaurant, which managed to feel both exotically Californian and comfortably local. There was no turning back: we had seen the future of dining, and it was relaxed, affordable and inviting.

The downstairs Unicorn Pub has been a Calgary landmark for forty years, but it wasn't until the Rose and Crown Pub opened in 1986 that we were in for the British Invasion. The Rose and Crown hired local rugby players as barmen, had a large selection of beers on tap and served a wide menu that included salads as well as fish and chips and steak and kidney pie. The Ship and Anchor Pub opened in 1990, and the popularity of its Saturday-afternoon jam, weeknight bands, inexpensive menu items and sunny patio has never waned. People regularly line up around the block to get in, and at least two generations of Calgarians have consumed its chicken wings, curry, Ship Burgers and countless pints of beer. There have been many imitators, but the Rose and the Ship remain our steadfast favourites.

A whole series of new dining options followed in the '90s. Our love affair with sushi really took off: sushi restaurants appeared on almost every block, and they are still always full. Italian food had always been popular, but when Mercato opened with a deli, market and restaurant all under one roof and introduced family-style dining, it became so popular that they had to expand the restaurant. And recently it's become clear that we like to go for breakfast, which has resulted in several excellent diners—most of which feature the Bloody Caesar, the drink Walter Chell invented in Calgary in 1969 at what is now The Westin Hotel.

Today, the city boasts one of the most exciting culinary scenes in the country. Recent economic booms have attracted award-winning chefs, restaurateurs and cooks from all over the world. Many of Calgary's long-established restaurateurs like Sal Howell of River Café, and chefs Judy Wood of Meez Fast Home Cuisine, Glen Manzer of Bonterra Trattoria, and Kyle Groves of Catch & The Oyster Bar, to name just a few, have mentored and encouraged young chefs to push themselves and try new ideas. By travelling and working internationally, our chefs have returned with a new outlook about shopping and sourcing seasonal, regional, ethically produced meat and produce to support local businesses and give us the best food choices available.

Thanks to our boom-and-bust economy, we're always aware that the good times can suddenly end and only the strong will survive. This drive toward creativity, reinvention and self-reliance has resulted in a local food scene that's never been more exciting in terms of variety, quality and uniqueness. *Calgary Cooks* offers you the opportunity to create recipes from many of this city's best restaurants. Along with new twists on old favourites, like bacon and French toast, the eighty featured recipes are fresh, contemporary and designed to be made in the comfort of your own kitchen. Showcasing the best of our local ingredients, and the creativity and skill of our chefs, these dishes reflect respect for our surroundings and our constantly evolving food scene.

Don't wait! Start cooking, and have fun!

List of Recipes

THE RECIPES

Guacamole

SERVES 6 TO 8

Our signature dish brings the fresh vibrancy of Mexico into your kitchen and onto your plate. Be creative and personalize this recipe with your favourite combination of chili peppers. We use a mixture of 80 per cent serrano and 20 per cent jalapeño peppers, but any combination is fine; just remove the seeds and stems and chop the peppers to a fine dice. Use gloves while you do this, make sure to wash your hands thoroughly, and don't touch your eyes or your face because the pepper juices will burn. Serve premium tortilla chips with this sublime dip.

1 tsp kosher salt

3 Tbsp finely diced white onions

3 Tbsp chopped Roma tomatoes

3 Tbsp chopped fresh cilantro

2 tsp chopped garlic

1 to 2 Tbsp seeded, finely chopped jalapeño or serrano peppers

2 avocados

2 limes, in wedges

1 large bag premium tortilla chips

In a medium bowl, combine salt, onions, tomatoes, cilantro, garlic and chili peppers until well mixed. Cut avocados in half, remove the pits and scoop the flesh into the mixing bowl. Discard the pits and peels. Squeeze lime juice over the avocados, and, using two forks, mash the avocados into the onion-tomato mixture until the guacamole is slightly chunky. Adjust the seasonings by adding more salt or a squeeze more lime, if necessary. Serve immediately with tortilla chips.

Churros

SERVES 4 TO 6

1 cup water
⅓ cup butter
2 packed Tbsp brown sugar
½ tsp salt
1 cup all-purpose flour
1 egg
½ tsp vanilla extract
8 cups peanut, sunflower,
    canola or grapeseed oil,
    for deep frying
¼ cup icing sugar
1 Tbsp ground cinnamon
1 ½ tsp cayenne pepper

Never stand in line for these delicious fritters again. This recipe gives you the power to make churros a reality, right in your own kitchen. Serve them hot, after a dinner of Family-style Lamb Barbacoa (page 120), with a ramekin of dulce de leche or chocolate sauce (see page 34 for a white chocolate ganache) for dipping.

Bring water to a boil in a medium saucepan on high. Stir in butter, brown sugar and salt. As soon as the sugar and salt have dissolved, add flour all at once, while stirring vigorously with a wooden spoon. Lower the heat to medium and stir the mixture until it forms a ball, about 5 minutes. Remove from the heat and allow to cool for a few minutes. Add egg and vanilla and mix well until thoroughly incorporated. Scoop the dough into a pastry bag fitted with a star tip.

Line a baking sheet with waxed paper, parchment or a silicone mat. Pipe 6-inch-long strips of batter onto the lined baking sheet and refrigerate for about 10 minutes to allow the mixture to firm up. (You should have about 8 churros.)

Line a plate with paper towels. Half-fill a deep pot with peanut (or other) oil and heat on high to 350°F, about 10 minutes. (Use a deep-fat thermometer to check the temperature. Alternatively, drop a piece of batter in the oil, and if it sizzles, it's ready.) Using a slotted spoon or tongs, carefully drop churros into the hot oil and cook for 5 to 7 minutes, until golden. Transfer to the paper towel–lined plate to drain.

In a wide, shallow bowl, combine icing sugar, cinnamon and cayenne until well mixed. Toss the churros in the sugar mixture while still hot. Eat immediately and enjoy.

Dolsot Bibimbap
(Mixed Rice with Vegetables)

SERVES 4

3 cups short-grain rice

2 zucchinis, julienned

Salt and black pepper

2 Tbsp butter

3 Tbsp vegetable or canola oil

4 king oyster mushrooms,
  thinly sliced

3 cloves garlic, minced

2 red bell peppers, cut
  lengthwise in ¼-inch slices

2 carrots, julienned

Zest and juice of 1 lime

3 cups soybean sprouts

1 tsp granulated sugar

¼ cup + 1 tsp sesame oil,
  plus more for garnish

1 tsp sesame seeds, roasted,
  plus more for garnish

3 cups fresh corn (4 medium-sized
  ears of corn with kernels cut
  off and cobs discarded)

1 tsp gochugaru (Korean chili flakes)

1 Tbsp white vinegar

4 eggs

1 cup chopped pea shoots,
  for garnish

2 or 3 green onions chopped,
  for garnish

¼ cup gochujang (Korean
  red pepper paste)

In Korean, *bibim* means "mixing" and *bap* means "rice." This popular dish is a large bowl of rice topped with a variety of vegetables that have been individually prepared and are then mixed in at the table, just as the dish is being served. It is sometimes served in a hot *dolsot*, or stone bowl, which gives the bottom layer of rice a nice crispy texture and causes the vegetables to sizzle as they're mixed. If you don't have four dolsots, use regular bowls (but you won't get the crispy rice at the bottom). Bibimbap originated as a way of using up leftovers and is often served with *gochujang* (Korean red pepper paste), which, along with *gochugaru* (Korean chili flakes) and soybean sprouts, can be found at T & T, Superstore, Arirang Oriental Food Store and other specialty food stores.

In a rice cooker or a saucepan, cook rice according to the package instructions, using slightly less water than is called for—the rice for bibimbap should be a little dry for best results. While the rice is cooking, prepare the vegetables.

Place the zucchinis in a large bowl, generously sprinkle with salt and allow to sit for 10 to 15 minutes.

While the zucchinis are resting, melt 1 Tbsp of the butter with 1 Tbsp of the vegetable (or canola) oil in a frying pan on high heat. Add mushrooms and ⅓ of the garlic, season with a pinch of salt and black pepper, and sauté for about 5 minutes, or until mushrooms are softened. Using a slotted spoon, transfer mushrooms to a bowl, cover with a plate, set aside and add 1 Tbsp of oil to the pan. Stir in bell peppers, season with a pinch of salt and black pepper, and sauté for about 5 minutes, until softened. Using a slotted spoon, transfer peppers to a bowl, cover them with a plate and set aside. Add the remaining 1 Tbsp oil to the pan and increase the heat to medium-high. Stir in carrots and season to taste with salt and black pepper and sauté for 1 to 2 minutes. Remove from the heat and set aside.

Using your hands, squeeze out (and discard) any excess liquid from the zucchinis and return them to the bowl. Add lime zest and juice and ⅓ of the garlic and season with black pepper to taste.

Bring a large pot of salted water to a boil on high heat. Add soybean sprouts and blanch for 3 minutes. Using a slotted spoon, transfer them to a colander to drain well. Transfer sprouts to a large bowl. Add sugar, 1 tsp of the sesame oil, ½ tsp of the sesame seeds and the remaining garlic, toss well and season to taste with salt and black pepper. Add the corn to the boiling water, cook for 1 minute, then drain it well and transfer to a bowl. Stir in gochugaru, the remaining 1 Tbsp butter and ½ tsp of sesame seeds and toss well. Season to taste with salt and black pepper.

Bring a small pot of water to a gentle simmer. Use a thermometer to check the temperature of the water; ideally, it should be 145°F. Add white vinegar and use a fork to swirl the water in a clockwise direction, then crack the eggs, one at a time, into the simmering liquid. Cook for 45 seconds and gently use a slotted spoon to scoop them up and transfer them to a plate. (Alternatively, pan-fry the eggs sunny side up.)

To serve the bibimbap, heat the stone bowls in the oven at 350°F until hot, about 5 minutes. In each bowl, place 1 Tbsp sesame oil and ¼ of the rice and allow them cook for a few minutes, until the rice sizzles. Do not stir. Using a spoon, make a small indentation in the middle of the rice and put an egg into it. Arrange vegetables over the rice, leaving the yolk exposed. Drizzle each serving with sesame oil. Garnish with pea shoots, green onions and sesame seeds and serve with gochujang.

Daeji Bulgogi (Grilled Spicy Pork Blade Steaks with Sesame Slaw)

SERVES 4

In Korean, *daeji* means "pork" and *bulgogi* means "fire meat." Living up to its name, this dish is made with a marinade of *gochujang* (Korean red pepper paste) and lots of fresh garlic and ginger. Grated apple adds a vibrant sweetness that lifts the flavours. You can use any cut of pork for this dish; we recommend a slightly fatty pork shoulder or belly. Look for gochujang and *gochugaru* (Korean chili flakes) at T & T, Arirang Oriental Food Store in Calgary and most specialty food stores.

GRILLED SPICY STEAKS In a medium bowl, combine gochujang, gochugaru, soy sauce, sesame oil, garlic, ginger, apple, lime zest and juice and brown sugar until well mixed. Place pork in a large resealable plastic bag, add marinade and seal. Shake the bag to ensure pork is thoroughly coated, then refrigerate and allow steaks to marinate overnight, or for at least 4 hours.

SESAME SLAW In a large bowl, toss cabbages, carrots and green onions. In a smaller bowl, whisk mayonnaise with sesame oil, rice vinegar, sugar, soy sauce and sesame seeds. Using tongs or a rubber spatula, toss vegetables with the dressing until well coated. Season to taste with salt and black pepper.

FINISH STEAKS Preheat a barbecue or grill to medium-hot. Pour off and discard the marinade from the steaks. Grill steaks for about 4 minutes per side for medium rare. Transfer to individual plates and serve immediately with a side of sesame slaw.

GRILLED SPICY STEAKS

½ cup gochujang (Korean red pepper paste)

2 tsp gochugaru (Korean chili flakes)

2 Tbsp soy sauce

1 Tbsp sesame oil

4 cloves garlic, minced

1 Tbsp minced fresh ginger

½ Granny Smith apple, cored and julienned

Zest and juice of 3 limes

¼ cup brown sugar

4 pork shoulder blade steaks, each 9 oz

SESAME SLAW

1 head green cabbage, thinly sliced

½ cup thinly sliced red cabbage

2 carrots, thinly sliced

2 green onions, thinly sliced

1 cup mayonnaise

2 Tbsp sesame oil

1 Tbsp rice vinegar

1 Tbsp granulated sugar

1 tsp soy sauce

2 Tbsp sesame seeds

Salt and black pepper

Wild Mushroom Tart

SERVES 6 AS AN APPETIZER

TART PASTRY
2 cups all-purpose flour,
   plus more for dusting
1 cup (½ lb) unsalted butter, cold
½ cup sour cream
Salt

MUSHROOM FILLING
1 Tbsp butter
1 Tbsp olive oil
1 cup chopped wild or cremini
   mushrooms
2 shallots, very finely minced
Pinch of chopped fresh thyme
   leaves
3 Tbsp dry sherry
¾ cup whipping cream
¾ cup vegetable stock
Grated parmesan, for garnish
Microgreens, for garnish

This tart is perfect as both a starter and a brunch item. Add a green salad and it's excellent as a light lunch. Versatile and delicious, it has the appearance of a quiche, but blind-baking the pastry and adding the cooked filling later make for a texturally superior dish. The crust is crispy and the filling is creamy and delicious. Use wild mushrooms, such as chanterelles or morels, or domestic mushrooms as available.

TART PASTRY Place flour in a large bowl. Using a handheld grater, grate butter into the flour and mix with your fingers until it becomes a coarse meal. Add sour cream and a pinch of salt and mix gently until a dough just forms. Be sure not to overwork the dough or it will become tough. Bring the dough together into a ball, cover it with plastic wrap and refrigerate for at least 30 minutes or as long as overnight.

When you're ready to make the tarts, preheat the oven to 375°F. Dust six 4-inch tart pans with flour and cut six rounds of parchment paper or aluminum foil big enough to fit in the bottom of the tart pans. Have on hand enough dried beans or pie weights to cover the bottom of each of the pans.

Lightly dust a work surface with flour. Divide the dough into six pieces and roll them out individually to a thickness of ⅛ inch. Press the dough into each pan, cover it with a circle of parchment paper (or foil) and arrange the beans or pie weights on top to help keep the pastry from rising while it bakes. Arrange the tart pans on a baking sheet and cook for 10 minutes. Remove the tart pans from the oven and reduce the oven temperature to 350°F. Using an oven mitt, gently tip the beans or pie weights out of the tart pans and discard the parchment paper (or foil). Return the pastry to the oven and bake the tart shells for another 15 minutes, or until golden. Remove from the oven and allow to cool.

MUSHROOM FILLING In a sauté pan on high heat, melt butter into the olive oil, add mushrooms and sauté until golden, about 15 minutes. Add shallots and thyme and sauté until softened, about 5 minutes. Deglaze the pan with sherry, scraping the bottom of the pan to release any of the browned bits, then add cream and vegetable stock. Turn down the heat to medium and gently reduce the mixture to a thick, creamy paste, 5 to 10 minutes.

TO ASSEMBLE Preheat the oven to 425°F. Reheat the tart shells for 3 minutes, then remove them from the oven and divide the warm mushroom filling evenly among them. Garnish with grated parmesan and microgreens and serve immediately.

Warm Golden Beet and Arugula Salad

SERVES 6 TO 8

3 lbs golden beets, washed and greens removed

1 ½ cups white vinegar

½ cup granulated sugar

1 Tbsp kosher salt

½ cinnamon stick

2 ⅓ Tbsp olive oil

2 shallots, sliced

½ cup vegetable stock

2 Tbsp white balsamic vinegar

2 oz fresh goat cheese, crumbled

Salt

6 to 8 generous handfuls of arugula, washed and spun dry

Handful of pumpkin seeds, toasted, for garnish

3 blood oranges, in segments, for garnish

Thanks to hothouse farming, golden beets are available throughout the year and can be found at most supermarkets. One of the great things about these beets is that they won't stain your fingers purple. The beets' golden colour also adds visual impact, and their mellow flavour complements peppery, nutty arugula. Perfect as an accompaniment to the Wild Mushroom Tart (page 18), the golden beet and arugula salad goes well with pasta, lamb and fish as well. Tangelos, mandarins or regular oranges can be substituted if blood oranges are unavailable.

In a large pot combine beets, white vinegar, sugar, salt and cinnamon stick. Add enough water to completely cover the beets. Bring to a boil on high, then reduce the heat to medium, cooking the beets for about 30 minutes, or until they can be pierced easily with a fork. Remove the pan from the heat, allow the beets to cool in the liquid, then peel and cut them into bite-sized pieces. Discard the cooking liquid and beet skins.

Heat 1 Tbsp of the olive oil in a large sauté pan on medium, add shallots and cook until translucent, about 10 minutes. Add beets and let them heat through. Using a slotted spoon, transfer beets and shallots to a large bowl and set aside.

Deglaze the pan with vegetable stock, scraping the flavourful beet and shallot bits stuck to the bottom of the pan until they dissolve. Reduce the heat to medium-low and let the sauce simmer for about 20 minutes, reducing it by ½. Stir in balsamic vinegar, increase the heat to high and bring the mixture to a boil. Immediately turn off the heat and stir in the goat cheese. Allow it to melt before adding the remaining 1⅓ Tbsp olive oil and a pinch of salt.

Add arugula to the warm beet and shallot mixture and toss gently. Divide the salad evenly among individual plates, then garnish with pumpkin seeds and blood oranges. Serve immediately.

Brined Pork Belly

SERVES 6 TO 8

Don't just bring home the bacon—make it from scratch! The hardest thing about this recipe is waiting the 16 hours for the pork to brine and cook. Curing salts are often used to preserve food and prevent it from spoiling. They also tint the meat and keep it looking pink. We use curing salt and nitricure, which is available from DnR Sausage Supplies in Calgary. You can use less expensive coarse-ground sel gris instead. Serve this bacon at brunch with Chocolate Milk French Toast (page 23)—you'll have more than enough for several goes!

⅓ cup pickling spice

2 cups kosher salt

3 cups granulated sugar

⅓ cup curing salt or sel gris

⅓ cup black peppercorns

1 cup minced garlic
(about 4 bulbs)

4 bay leaves

4 sprigs fresh rosemary

10 cups water

1 skinless pork belly,
5 to 6 lbs, in one piece

In a large pot, combine pickling spice, salt, sugar, curing salt (or sel gris), peppercorns, garlic, bay leaves, rosemary and water. Cover and bring to a boil on high heat. Once the salt and sugar are dissolved, remove the brine from the heat and allow it to cool completely.

Pour the cold brine into a container large enough to hold the pork. Add the pork, cover and refrigerate for no longer than 10 hours. (Brining the pork longer may make it too salty.)

Preheat the oven to 200°F. Remove pork from the brine, rinse it well under cold water and pat dry. Discard the brine. Lay the meat flat on a baking sheet or in a roasting pan, cover with aluminum foil and roast for 6 hours. Remove from the oven and allow it to rest for 1 hour. (The resting time allows the muscle fibres to relax and reabsorb moisture, which makes the bacon more tender and juicy.)

Line a plate with paper towels. Heat a frying pan on medium-high. Cut pork in ¼-inch slices and fry until golden and crispy, about 3 minutes per side. Using tongs, transfer the cooked bacon to the paper towel–lined plate to drain. You've made bacon!

Chocolate Milk French Toast with Almond Butter

SERVES 6 TO 8

French toast is easy to make for a decadent brunch; however, remember to soak the bread the night before you want to serve this dish. Pair it with Brined Pork Belly bacon (page 21) to really impress your friends and family.

FRENCH TOAST Lightly grease a large casserole dish with butter. Arrange the bread slices in a single layer, squeezing in as many as possible.

In a large bowl, whisk together the eggs, chocolate milk, cream and cinnamon. Slice the vanilla bean lengthwise and scrape the seeds into the custard mixture (or add the vanilla paste). Mix well. Pour the custard over the bread slices, ensuring that they are totally submerged. Cover the dish with plastic wrap and refrigerate overnight.

Half an hour before you plan to serve the French toast, preheat the oven to 375°F. Combine butter, brown sugar and honey in a small saucepan on high heat and bring to a boil. Reduce the heat to low and simmer until the sugar is dissolved. Set aside and allow to cool slightly.

ALMOND BUTTER Place butter, lemon juice and honey in a medium bowl. Using a handheld mixer or a whisk, beat until smooth and well combined. Fold in the almonds and cinnamon and season with a pinch of salt. Set aside.

FINISH FRENCH TOAST Remove the soaked bread from the fridge and unwrap the dish. Drizzle about ¼ cup of the warm syrup mixture over the bread, ensuring you reach all slices. (Reserve the remaining syrup to serve at the table.) Bake for 30 minutes, or until bread is brown and crispy. Serve immediately with a generous dollop of almond butter on top.

FRENCH TOAST

¾ cup butter, plus more
    for greasing
1 loaf artisanal bread of
    your choice, in thick slices
8 eggs
2 cups chocolate milk
1 ½ cups whipping cream
¼ tsp ground cinnamon
1 vanilla bean or ½ tsp vanilla paste
1 ⅓ cups brown sugar
3 Tbsp honey

ALMOND BUTTER

½ cup (¼ lb) butter, room
    temperature
Juice of 1 lemon
2 Tbsp honey
⅓ cup slivered almonds, toasted
Pinch of ground cinnamon
Salt

Savoury Leek and Gruyère Soufflé

SERVES 8

1 Tbsp + ½ cup (¼ lb) unsalted
   butter, room temperature,
   plus more for greasing
1 cup finely grated parmesan
1 leek, white part only, finely diced
2 ¾ cups whole milk
½ yellow onion,
   studded with 3 cloves
1 bay leaf
⅔ cup all-purpose flour
½ cup grated Gruyère
6 egg yolks
6 egg whites
1 cup whipping cream (optional)

Light, savoury and perfect for brunch or lunch. Serve this soufflé with a Warm Golden Beet and Arugula Salad (page 20) and a light red, or dry sparkling, wine.

Preheat the oven to 350°F. Using a pastry brush, lightly grease eight 8-oz ramekins with butter. Refrigerate the ramekins until chilled, then butter them again and dust them lightly with parmesan. (Do this by putting a generous amount of cheese into a ramekin, tapping it around the edges to distribute the cheese evenly, then pouring the excess cheese into the next ramekin. Repeat until all ramekins have been prepared. Reserve the excess parmesan for use later in the recipe.)

Melt 1 Tbsp of the butter in a large frying pan on medium heat. Add leeks and sauté gently until soft but not browned, about 10 minutes. Drain off the liquid, then transfer leeks to a plate and set aside. Reserve the pan.

Place a fine-mesh sieve over a small bowl. In a small saucepan, scald milk with the onion and bay leaf on medium heat for about 5 minutes to infuse the milk with their flavour. Allow the mixture to cool slightly, then pour the milk through the sieve. Discard the onion and bay leaf.

Melt the remaining ½ cup butter in the reserved pan on medium-high heat. Stir in flour, letting it cook for a few minutes. Reduce the heat to medium and gradually whisk in the scalded milk, a bit at a time, until all of the milk is incorporated. Add Gruyère and stir until completely incorporated. Remove from the heat, beat in the egg yolks and add the reserved leeks. Set aside.

In the bowl of a stand mixer, whip egg whites until they form firm peaks (add a pinch of salt to stabilize them). Gently stir ¼ of the egg whites into the cheese and egg yolk mixture, then fold in the remaining egg whites. Divide the soufflé batter evenly among the ramekins, making sure to clean the edges carefully. (Messy edges may prevent the soufflés from rising properly.)

Set the ramekins in a large roasting pan. Boil enough water to half-fill the pan and pour in enough to reach about halfway up the ramekins. Bake for 30 minutes, until the soufflés are firm to the touch. Remove from the oven, then gently lift the ramekins from the hot water and allow them to cool slightly. Run a sharp knife around the edges of the ramekins to loosen the soufflés, then gently invert them onto a baking sheet. Refrigerate until chilled.

Preheat the oven to 375°F. Remove the soufflés from the fridge and bake for 8 minutes. While they're baking, scald the cream (if using) in a small saucepan on medium-high heat. Remove the soufflés from the oven and increase the oven temperature to broil. Arrange the warm soufflés in individual bowls, cover with a generous tablespoonful of parmesan and the scalded cream, then broil the soufflés until their tops are golden, about 10 seconds. Serve hot.

SERVES 10

Braised Rabbit Legs with Ricotta Gnocchi, Chanterelles and Two Mustards

CLARIFIED BUTTER

½ cup (¼ lb) unsalted butter

BRAISED RABBIT LEGS

10 rabbit legs

Salt

6 shallots, thinly sliced

1 cup white wine vinegar

1 bottle (750 mL) white wine

6 Tbsp Dijon mustard

6 cups chicken stock

2 cups whipping cream

4 sprigs fresh thyme

2 bay leaves

4 cloves garlic, minced

2 Tbsp butter

2 cups fresh chanterelle
   (or cremini) mushrooms

1 tsp grainy mustard

Ask your butcher to cut up and clean the rabbit for you, as this will save time and simplify your preparation. Or make the dish with chicken thighs, if you prefer. Prepare the gnocchi while the rabbit is cooking. Serve this recipe for dinner, with a full-bodied French white wine.

CLARIFIED BUTTER Melt butter in a heavy saucepan on low heat and simmer until the foam rises to the top. Using a spoon, skim off the foam. Place a fine-mesh sieve over a frying pan and strain the butter into a jar, discarding the solids. Will keep refrigerated in an airtight container for up to 3 months.

BRAISED RABBIT LEGS Season rabbit legs with a little salt. Heat clarified butter in a large, heavy-bottomed casserole dish on medium-high. Add rabbit legs and lightly brown on all sides, about 5 minutes. Transfer rabbit to a large plate, cover and set aside.

Increase the heat to high. Add shallots to the casserole pan and cook until they start to release their water, about 5 minutes, turning down the heat to ensure that they don't burn or become too brown. Cover the pan, reduce the heat to medium-low and cook until shallots are soft and translucent but not brown, about 10 minutes. Pour in white wine vinegar and reduce by ⅔, then add white wine and reduce again by ⅔, about 15 minutes total. Stir in the regular Dijon, chicken stock, cream, thyme, bay leaves and garlic. Increase the heat to medium-high, bring the liquid to a boil and then immediately remove it from the heat. Return the rabbit legs to the casserole pan, cover and cook gently on medium heat for about 45 minutes, until the meat falls easily from the bone.

Continued overleaf…

RICOTTA GNOCCHI

1 lb ricotta, hung in cheesecloth overnight and drained

2 eggs

Salt

Pinch of freshly grated nutmeg

1 cup all-purpose flour, plus more for dusting

1 Tbsp unsalted butter

RICOTTA GNOCCHI In a large bowl, combine ricotta, eggs, a pinch of salt and nutmeg. Gradually add flour, using just enough to create a smooth dough. (You will probably not need the entire cup of flour.) Gather dough into a ball, wrap it in plastic wrap and refrigerate for 1 hour.

Lightly dust a clean work surface with flour. Remove the dough from the fridge, unwrap it and, rolling it back and forth between your palms, create long ropes about ¾ inch thick. Set them on the counter and cut them into evenly sized "pillows" about ½ inch wide.

FINISH RABBIT Using a slotted spoon, carefully remove the rabbit legs from the casserole and transfer them to a large bowl.

Melt butter in a frying pan on high heat. Add mushrooms and sauté until all the moisture has been released and evaporated, about 10 minutes. (The mushrooms should be slightly golden.)

Place a fine-mesh sieve over a clean saucepan, then pour the braising liquid through the sieve. Discard the solids. Set the braising liquid on medium-high heat, add the mushrooms and reduce by ½, about 20 minutes. Remove from the heat and stir in grainy mustard to taste. Add rabbit legs, return to the heat and warm through.

FINISH GNOCCHI Bring a large pot of salted water to a boil on high heat. Add gnocchi (in batches, if necessary) and boil until they start to float to the top, about 4 minutes. Using a slotted spoon, transfer the cooked gnocchi to a plate.

Melt butter in a frying pan on medium heat. Add the blanched gnocchi and sauté until golden.

TO ASSEMBLE Arrange gnocchi in the centre of a large family-style platter. Carefully place the braised rabbit legs on top of the gnocchi, ladle over the reduced braising liquid and mushrooms and serve immediately.

Wild Boar Carbonara

SERVES 4 TO 6

Liven up this classic pasta dish with the addition of bacon made from wild boar. Serve it for dinner and have the leftovers for breakfast. Wild boar bacon is available at specialty meat shops, but use double-smoked bacon if you prefer.

Place bacon in a large frying pan on medium heat and cook until bacon fat starts to melt, about 5 minutes. Stir in garlic, shallots, duck fat and olive oil and sauté for about 5 minutes, until garlic and shallots are translucent and about to caramelize. Season with a pinch of salt and black pepper.

Bring a large pot of salted water to a boil on high heat. Stir in pasta and cook according to the package directions until just "al dente," or slightly firm. Drain the pasta and set aside.

Add chili flakes to the shallot mixture, then deglaze the pan with white wine, and add the lemon juice and butter. Allow the butter to melt completely, stir well and remove from the heat. Using a spatula, fold in the pasta and return the pan to low heat. Gently toss the pasta with the shallot mixture until well coated. Sprinkle with Grana Padano. Pour in the eggs and mix them in gently. The sauce should thicken as the egg cooks with the heat from the cooked pasta. If the sauce becomes too thick, thin it with a little water or white wine. Adjust the seasonings, if necessary.

Spoon the pasta into a large family-style serving platter and garnish with more Grana Padano, parsley and a drizzle of olive oil. Serve immediately: carbonara waits for no one!

1 cup wild boar bacon, in ¼-inch dice
4 cloves garlic, sliced
½ cup sliced shallots
3 Tbsp duck fat
¼ cup extra-virgin olive oil, plus more for garnish
Salt and black pepper
¾ lb linguine or spaghetti
Pinch of chili flakes
¼ cup white wine
Juice of 1 lemon
¼ cup butter
1 ½ cups finely grated Grana Padano, plus more for garnish
2 eggs, lightly beaten
1 Tbsp chopped fresh Italian parsley, for garnish

Veal Meatballs

SERVES 4

Homemade meatballs are simply the best. Use your favourite tomato sauce to braise them, then serve these meatballs with crusty bread and a glass of Chianti.

Heat 2 Tbsp of the olive oil in a large sauté pan on medium-high. Add shallots and garlic, season with a pinch of salt and cook for 10 minutes. Remove from the heat, stir in cinnamon, fennel seeds and chili flakes and allow to cool completely.

Pour milk into a large bowl, add the bread and allow to soak for 10 minutes. Drain and discard the milk, then, using your hands, squeeze any excess liquid from the bread. Stir the bread mixture into the shallots and garlic. Add sage, oregano, basil, parsley, thyme, lemon zest and ground veal and mix gently until just combined. Do not overmix. Season with a pinch of salt and black pepper.

Heat 2 Tbsp of the olive oil in a large frying pan on high. Pinch off a quarter-sized piece of the meat mixture, form it into a patty and fry for 5 minutes, or until crisp and browned. Taste, and adjust the seasonings if necessary. Using your hands, shape the remaining meat mixture into 3-inch balls. Add 2 Tbsp more olive oil to the frying pan and carefully add meatballs, cooking them in batches, if necessary, until browned on all sides, 10 to 15 minutes. (Handle the meat gently so that you do not break up the balls.) Using a slotted spoon, transfer meatballs to a large ovenproof dish, arranging them in a single layer.

Preheat the oven to 400°F. Cover the meatballs with tomato sauce and bake for 30 minutes. Remove from the oven, arrange on a large family-style serving platter and garnish with parmesan and Italian parsley (or chopped basil or micro basil). Drizzle with olive oil and serve immediately.

6 Tbsp extra-virgin olive oil, plus more for garnish

½ cup finely diced shallots

6 cloves garlic, minced

Kosher salt and black pepper

Pinch of ground cinnamon

Pinch of ground fennel seeds

Pinch of chili flakes

2 cups whole milk

1 loaf fresh focaccia, crusts removed, roughly torn

1 tsp finely chopped fresh sage

1 tsp finely chopped fresh oregano

1 Tbsp finely chopped fresh basil or micro basil, plus more for garnish

1 Tbsp finely chopped fresh Italian parsley, plus more for garnish

1 tsp finely chopped fresh thyme leaves

Zest of 1 lemon

1 ¼ lbs ground veal

3 cups tomato sauce

1 cup grated parmesan

Orange Almond Lavender Torte

**SERVES 12
(MAKES ONE 10-INCH TORTE)**

BLACKBERRY COMPOTE

2 ½ cups fresh or frozen
    blackberries

½ cup granulated sugar
    or berry sugar

3 Tbsp water

3 Tbsp orange juice

CHANTILLY CREAM

1 cup whipping cream, chilled

½ tsp vanilla extract

1 Tbsp granulated sugar

ORANGE ALMOND TORTE

½ cup all-purpose flour

½ tsp baking powder

¼ cup finely ground almonds

¾ cup unsalted butter, room
    temperature

¾ cup granulated sugar

9 oz almond paste (Odense
    brand is very good), in
    ½-inch pieces

4 eggs

½ tsp vanilla extract

1 Tbsp Grand Marnier

Zest of 1 orange

1 Tbsp dried organic
    lavender blossoms

Rich and moist, this simple torte with a coarse crumb is ever so satisfying. Organic lavender creates a lovely, subtle flavour, but omit it if it doesn't appeal and you will still have the most wonderful dessert. (You can find lavender blossoms at specialty food and health food stores.) Perfect for holiday entertaining, the torte can be made up to two weeks ahead and kept, well wrapped, in the freezer. The torte is delicious on its own but is made more special with the toppings. The blackberry compote and Chantilly cream can also be made ahead, but assemble the cake just before serving.

BLACKBERRY COMPOTE In a small saucepan on medium heat, combine 1 ½ cups of the berries, sugar, water and orange juice. Simmer, stirring often, until berries start to break down, about 10 minutes. Add the remaining 1 cup berries, increase the heat to medium-high, and simmer, stirring the mixture until the compote coats the back of a spoon, about 10 minutes. Remove from the heat. Transfer to a non-reactive bowl, cover and refrigerate for up to 3 days. Serve warm or chilled.

CHANTILLY CREAM Place cream in the bowl of a stand mixer. Add vanilla and sugar and whip at high speed until the cream forms soft peaks (the cream should hold its shape but not be stiff), about 5 minutes. Cover and refrigerate for up to 2 hours.

ORANGE ALMOND TORTE Preheat the oven to 375°F. Line a 10-inch round springform pan with parchment paper and grease the sides lightly with nonstick baking spray.

In a small bowl, stir together flour, baking powder and almonds and set aside.

Place butter and sugar in the bowl of a stand mixer and, using the whisk attachment, combine at high speed until light and fluffy, about 3 minutes. With the motor running on low, add almond paste a bit at a time, scraping down the sides of the bowl to incorporate all ingredients into the batter (it does not have to be uniform).

On low to medium speed, add the eggs, one at a time, ensuring that each one is mixed in before adding the next one. Stir in the vanilla, Grand Marnier, orange zest and lavender. Using a spatula, scrape down the sides of the bowl.

With the motor running on low speed, gradually add the dry ingredients to the butter mixture until just combined. (Do not overmix the batter.) Pour the batter into the prepared pan and bake for 40 to 50 minutes, or until a knife inserted in the middle comes out clean and the cake is pulling away slightly from the sides of the pan. Remove from the oven and allow to cool in the pan for 30 minutes.

To serve, gently run a knife around the edges of the pan to loosen the cake. Release the top of the pan and gently slide the cake on its parchment onto a serving platter. To remove the parchment paper, place the base of the springform pan on top of the cake. Place one hand on the base atop the cake, and, with the other hand, lift the serving platter and gently invert the cake onto the springform base. Place the cake on the counter, base side down, lift up the serving platter and carefully peel the paper from the bottom of the torte. Discard the parchment paper. Replace the platter and, again, gently invert the cake with one hand on the base and the other on the serving platter. Remove the base. Cut the torte into slices and serve with dollops of Chantilly cream and blackberry compote.

Flourless Hazelnut Cake with White Chocolate Sour Cream Ganache and Raspberries

**SERVES 12
(MAKES ONE 8-INCH CAKE)**

WHITE CHOCOLATE SOUR CREAM GANACHE

1 lb roughly chopped white chocolate, preferably Callebaut, Lindt or Valrhona

1 cup sour cream (14% milk fat)

3 cups whipping cream, plus more, if needed

HAZELNUT CAKE

2 cups hazelnuts, toasted and skinned

1 tsp baking powder

3 Tbsp cornstarch

¾ cup granulated sugar

5 egg yolks

5 egg whites

2 cups fresh raspberries, washed and patted dry

¼ lb white chocolate, shaved, for garnish

¼ cup icing sugar, for garnish

Start this cake a day or two ahead of when you plan to serve it, as the ganache filling must be refrigerated to allow time for it to set up. Note that this recipe makes more ganache than you need for the cake, but it will keep in your fridge for a week. Use it to ice another cake or heat it up and thin it with a bit of cream to make a dip for Añejo's Churros (page 12). The cake layers can also be made a day ahead and wrapped in plastic, and you can assemble the cake a few hours before guests arrive and refrigerate it, covered, until you're ready to serve it. The assembled cake is best eaten the day it's made. For variety, make this cake with a combination of pistachios and almonds instead of hazelnuts, and serve it with strawberries or blackberries instead of the raspberries.

WHITE CHOCOLATE SOUR CREAM GANACHE In a 4-cup glass measuring cup or a large glass mixing bowl, melt white chocolate in the microwave on high for 1 minute. Whisk well and repeat microwaving and whisking until chocolate has melted completely, about 3 minutes. Pour in sour cream and whisk until well combined, then whisk in 1 cup of the whipping cream. Microwave the ganache on high heat for 4 to 5 minutes, until bubbly, then transfer it to a large bowl and whisk in the remaining 2 cups whipping cream until the mixture is thoroughly combined. Allow the ganache to cool to room temperature, cover with plastic wrap and refrigerate it for at least 8 hours.

HAZELNUT CAKE Preheat the oven to 350°F. Line two 8-inch cake or springform pans with parchment paper and grease the insides with nonstick baking spray.

In the bowl of a food processor, pulse hazelnuts with the baking powder and cornstarch until the nuts are finely chopped and the mixture is slightly coarse, not powdery. Set aside.

Continued overleaf…

In a large bowl of a stand mixer, beat ½ cup of the sugar and the egg yolks on high until the batter falls gently from the whisk in ribbons and the eggs are thick and a light lemon colour, about 3 minutes. Set aside.

In a second bowl, whip egg whites on high until they are slightly foamy, about 1 minute. With the motor running, gradually add the remaining ¼ cup sugar and beat until the whites form soft peaks, 1 to 2 minutes.

Using a spatula, gently fold ½ of the hazelnut mixture into the yolk and sugar mixture. When the mixtures are just combined, gently fold in the remaining hazelnut mixture. Next, fold in ½ of the egg whites until just combined, then gently fold in the remaining egg whites. Divide the batter equally between the two pans. (You should have about 3 cups of batter in each one.) Bake for 25 to 30 minutes (checking after 15 minutes), until the cakes are puffy and a knife inserted in the middle of each one comes out clean. Remove from the oven and allow to cool in the pans.

TO ASSEMBLE Gently run a sharp knife along the edge of each pan to loosen the cake. If you are using springform pans, release the top of the pan. To remove the parchment paper, place a plate on top of each cake. Place one hand on the plate atop the cake, and, with the other hand, lift the cake pan (or springform base) and gently invert the cake onto the plate. Place the cake on the counter and carefully peel the parchment paper from the bottom of each cake. Discard the parchment paper. Set the cakes aside.

Taste the chilled ganache. If you find it too rich, add ¼ cup whipping cream. (This is a case where adding more cream helps make it *less* rich.) In the bowl of a stand mixer, beat the ganache (and extra cream, if desired) on high, until it is thicker than whipped cream and just stiff enough to spread, 2 to 3 minutes. (Take care not to overbeat the ganache or it will separate and become grainy.)

Arrange one of the cakes, parchment-baked side up, on a serving platter. Using a spatula, spread ½ of the whipped ganache on the top of the cake and cover with a layer of raspberries. Set the other cake, parchment-baked side up, on top. Spread the remaining ganache on top and cover with more raspberries. Garnish with white chocolate shavings and dust lightly with icing sugar. Serve slightly chilled or at room temperature.

Crispy Calamari with Ancho Chili Mayo

SERVES 6

Customers have told us that this calamari recipe is the best ever. Calamari (squid) cooks quickly, making it delicious fast food. The flours can be found at Latin specialty stores, such as Salsita Mexican Food Market and Unimarket in Calgary. These flours are the secret to the incredible texture of this dish. Squid tubes are available at North Sea Fish, T & T and Superstore.

BREADED CALAMARI Place squid in a bowl and add milk. Cover and refrigerate for at least 3 hours to tenderize the meat.

While the squid is soaking, prepare the breading and the coconut topping. In a large mixing bowl, combine yucca, white corn and Maseca flours and set aside.

Preheat the oven to 350°F. Arrange the coconut on a baking sheet and toast until golden brown, about 5 minutes. Remove from the oven, allow to cool and reserve.

LIME SALT In a small bowl, mix together salt and lime zest.

ANCHO CHILI MAYO Place mayonnaise in a medium bowl. Stir in lime juice and chili powder, season with salt and refrigerate until needed.

FINISH BREADED CALAMARI Preheat canola (or other) oil to 350°F in a medium deep fryer or deep-sided pot. (Use a deep-fat thermometer to check the temperature.) Line a large plate with paper towels.

Drain the squid and discard the milk. Add the wet squid to the combined flours, and toss lightly until the seafood is completely coated and the flour has absorbed all the liquid. Shake off any excess flour.

Using a slotted spoon or tongs, gently lower squid into the hot oil in small batches, making sure it's completely submerged. Deep-fry until crispy, 3 to 4 minutes, then gently transfer to the paper towel–lined plate. Allow the oil to reheat, then repeat with the remaining squid.

Sprinkle the cooked calamari with lime salt, then arrange it on a platter or on individual serving plates. Drizzle with ancho chili mayo (or serve it in a bowl on the side) and top it with toasted coconut. Garnish with chili flakes and a wedge of lime.

BREADED CALAMARI

6 baby squid tubes, each 5 oz, in ½-inch rings

½ cup whole milk

½ cup yucca flour

½ cup white corn flour

½ cup Maseca corn flour

½ cup shredded sweetened coconut

8 cups canola, peanut, grapeseed or sunflower oil, for deep frying

Pinch of chili flakes, for garnish

1 lime, in 6 wedges, for garnish

LIME SALT

¼ cup kosher salt

Zest of 2 limes

ANCHO CHILI MAYO

1 cup mayonnaise

Juice of 1 lime

1 tsp ancho chili powder

Kosher salt

Tuna and Watermelon Ceviche

SERVES 6

This dish beautifully contrasts the textures of crispy watermelon and silky tuna. Aji amarillo, which is Spanish for "yellow chili," brings bright, flavourful Peruvian heat to the savoury, sweet and spicy ceviche. The paste can be found at Latin specialty food stores like Salsita Mexican Food Market and Unimarket in Calgary, but if you can't find it, Thai yellow curry paste works well as a substitute.

TOMATO AND CHILI SALSA Combine ingredients in a medium bowl and allow the flavours to blend for at least 30 minutes.

AJI AMARILLO COCONUT SAUCE Thoroughly combine coconut milk, aji amarillo paste (or Thai yellow curry paste) and sugar in a bowl and allow to sit for 30 minutes. Strain the sauce through a fine-mesh sieve, discard the solids and reserve. Season to taste with salt.

TUNA CEVICHE Using a sharp knife, carefully shave 24 slices, each ½ inch thick, from the tuna and season them with salt, black pepper and lemon juice. Allow to marinate for about 30 minutes.

Cut the watermelon into 2-inch squares. You should have at least 24 cubes.

TO ASSEMBLE On each of 6 plates, arrange a piece of watermelon in each quadrant. Season with salt and a grind or two of black pepper. Spoon a tablespoon of tomato and chili salsa between each piece of watermelon. Roll tuna into logs and place one, seam side down, on top of each spoonful of salsa. Drizzle the plates with aji amarillo coconut sauce and garnish with slices of radish. Serve immediately.

TOMATO AND CHILI SALSA

1 cup cherry tomatoes, halved
1 red bell pepper, finely diced
1 small red onion, finely diced
Juice of 2 lemons
¼ cup rice vinegar
1 Tbsp granulated sugar
¼ cup fresh mint, very thinly sliced
1 Tbsp aji amarillo paste (or Thai yellow curry paste)
½ Tbsp thinly sliced Thai red chilies
Pinch of salt

AJI AMARILLO COCONUT SAUCE

½ cup coconut milk
1 Tbsp aji amarillo paste (or Thai yellow curry paste)
2 Tbsp granulated sugar
Salt

TUNA CEVICHE

1 lb fresh tuna, centre cut
Salt and black pepper
Juice of 1 lemon
1 medium watermelon
4 radishes, thinly sliced

Dover Sole with Sauce Grenobloise

SERVES 4

2 shallots, finely diced
¼ cup finely minced fresh chives
2 Tbsp olive oil
1 lb fingerling potatoes
1 cup + 2 Tbsp butter
4 sole fillets, each ¼ lb
2 Tbsp capers, drained
Juice of 1 lemon
1 handful fresh Italian
　　parsley, chopped
1 lemon, in wedges, for garnish

Herbed potatoes and delicately flavoured butter-fried sole topped with a lemony, buttery, briny Grenobloise sauce—yum. Serve with a dry French Chablis for an elegantly impressive dinner.

In a medium bowl, combine shallots and chives, then add just enough olive oil to moisten them, about 1 Tbsp. Set aside. Bring a medium pot of salted water to a boil on medium-high heat. Peel potatoes and slice lengthwise, then add to the pot and cook until tender, about 15 minutes. Drain, add to the shallot-chive mixture and toss to coat. Cover and set aside.

Warm a large serving platter in the oven at 350°F. In a frying pan, heat the remaining 1 Tbsp olive oil and 2 Tbsp of the butter on medium-high. When the butter is browned, add sole in a single layer (cook in batches, if necessary). Cook for 3 minutes per side, then remove from the heat and transfer to the warmed serving platter.

To the frying pan, add the remaining 1 cup butter and all of the capers. Stir in lemon juice and parsley. Cook on medium-high heat until butter has melted and capers are sizzling. Pour the sauce over the sole. Garnish the platter with wedges of lemon, and serve with the potatoes.

Jerusalem Artichoke Soup

SERVES 4 TO 6

⅓ cup butter

1 leek, white part only, sliced

1 stalk celery, roughly chopped

1 yellow onion, roughly chopped

1 lb Jerusalem artichokes, peeled
and cut in ½-inch cubes

6 cups chicken stock

¾ cup whipping cream,
plus more for garnish

Salt and black pepper

¼ cup butter, cold, in
¼-inch cubes (optional)

The Jerusalem artichoke, also widely known as a sunchoke, is a vegetable with an earthy flavour. It's the root of a sunflower plant and tastes just like an artichoke heart. It can be found at supermarkets, farmers' markets and specialty food stores, usually in the fall. Serve this soup with fresh flatbread and olives.

Melt butter in a large pot on medium-low. Add leeks, celery and onions and cook gently until fragrant and translucent, about 15 minutes. Add Jerusalem artichokes and cook, stirring occasionally, for 3 minutes. Pour in chicken stock and allow the soup to simmer for 30 minutes.

Remove soup from the heat and allow it to cool slightly. Transfer it to a blender and process on high speed until very smooth. With the motor running, add cream in a continuous stream. Season to taste with salt and black pepper.

Ladle soup into individual bowls. Spoon a touch of cream and a couple of cubes of butter (if using) into each bowl. Serve hot.

SERVES 4

Pan-seared B.C. Halibut and Spot Prawns with Morel, English Pea and Chorizo Ragoût

½ lb cured chorizo sausage, in ¼-inch dice

2 Tbsp minced shallots

1 clove garlic, minced

¼ lb morel mushrooms, cleaned and patted dry

2 tsp + a pinch of fresh thyme leaves

¼ cup dry white wine

½ lb ratte or fingerling potatoes, boiled, peeled and cut in ½-inch-thick rounds

1 cup English peas, shelled and blanched

½ cup (¼ lb) butter, cold, in ½-inch cubes

Salt and black pepper

Juice of 2 lemons

¼ cup olive oil

4 wild halibut fillets, each 6 oz

12 large B.C. spot prawns, peeled

2 Tbsp minced fresh chives

Sprigs of watercress, for garnish

Timing is everything in this inspired dish of fresh halibut and spot prawns atop a chorizo ragoût made with small, nutty French ratte potatoes. The potatoes can be boiled in advance. The ragoût will finish cooking as the halibut emerges from the oven and the prawns hit the hot frying pan for a quick sizzle.

Place chorizo in a large saucepan on medium heat and cook until it releases its fat, 8 to 10 minutes. Add shallots and garlic and cook until tender, 10 minutes. Stir in morels, sautéing until softened, about 10 minutes, then add 2 tsp of the thyme. Slightly cool the pan with white wine. Gently add potatoes and peas and bring the mixture to a boil. Slowly stir in butter until the ragoût thickens, then season with salt, black pepper and lemon juice to taste. Remove from the heat, cover and set aside.

Preheat the oven to 400°F. Heat olive oil in a large cast-iron pan on high. Add halibut fillets all at once and sear on one side until golden brown, about 10 minutes. Do not turn the fish over. Bake halibut in the oven, in the cast-iron pan, for about 10 minutes, until the fish reaches 135°F, or fish flakes when touched with the tip of a knife. Transfer halibut to a plate and set aside.

Place the hot cast-iron pan on medium-high heat. Add prawns and a few thyme leaves and cook for 1 minute. Remove from the heat.

To serve, divide the chorizo ragoût among 4 warmed plates and sprinkle with the chives. Top each serving with a halibut fillet and 3 spot prawns, garnish with watercress and serve immediately.

Rhubarb-glazed Weathervane Scallops with Braised Bacon and Cabbage

SERVES 4

BRAISED BACON AND CABBAGE

2 lb slab of bacon (thickest piece available)

¼ cup olive oil

1 onion, chopped

4 cloves garlic, minced

2 fresh bay leaves

1 tsp black peppercorns

¼ cup fresh thyme sprigs

12 cups chicken stock

1 chunk parmesan rind, 4 to 6 inches long

2 Tbsp butter

2 heads Savoy cabbage, thinly shaved

¼ cup truffle honey (or ¼ cup honey mixed with 1 tsp black truffle paste)

RHUBARB-GLAZED SCALLOPS

2 cups rhubarb juice

2 cups granulated sugar

1 cup water

¼ cup chopped green onions

1 tsp chili flakes

1 tsp salt

1 Tbsp butter

2 Tbsp olive oil

12 large weathervane scallops

Bacon nirvana can be achieved, but it can't be rushed. The braised pork must be pressed overnight, so start this part of the recipe the day before you need it. Rhubarb, that wonderful sign of spring, is found in back alleys everywhere, so gather up a bunch and cook it slightly and then purée it in a blender or food processor and strain it to get the juice. Alternatively, Saskatoon Farm sells frozen rhubarb at farmers' markets. Smoked paprika and panko crumbs are available at Superstore, T & T and specialty food stores.

BRAISED BACON AND CABBAGE Preheat the oven to 400°F. Line a baking sheet with parchment paper.

Trim the skin off the fat cap of the bacon and discard. Pour olive oil into a deep-sided braising pan and heat on high until hot. Add onions and garlic and cook, stirring often, until fragrant and soft, about 10 minutes. Stir in bay leaves, peppercorns, thyme, chicken stock and cheese rind. Submerge bacon in this mixture, ensuring that it is covered by 1 inch of liquid. Cover the pot and cook in the oven for 3 ½ hours.

Using a long-handled fork, transfer bacon to the parchment paper–lined baking sheet. Cover bacon with another piece of parchment and a second baking sheet. Arrange several heavy cans or jars on top to press the bacon, and refrigerate overnight.

Strain the braising liquid into a saucepan, discarding the solids, and simmer it on medium heat until reduced by ⅔, 20 to 30 minutes. Allow the mixture to cool, cover and then refrigerate for up to 1 week. (You will have more than the ¼ cup you need for this recipe. Use the leftovers in any recipe that calls for stock.)

RHUBARB-GLAZED SCALLOPS In a large non-reactive pot, boil rhubarb juice, sugar, water, green onions, chili flakes and salt on medium-high heat until reduced by ½, about 15 minutes. Remove from the heat and allow to cool slightly. Place a fine-mesh sieve over a clean pot and strain the glaze. Discard the solids and set aside the glaze.

FINISH BACON AND CABBAGE In a large pan, heat butter on medium. Add cabbage and cook until it turns green and is wilted but still crunchy, 8 to 10 minutes. Add the ¼ cup of bacon braising liquid and cook until cabbage is tender, about 8 minutes. Remove from the heat and set aside to keep warm.

Remove bacon from the fridge, discard any pressed-out liquid and cut into eight 2-inch cubes. Heat a frying pan on medium-high, add bacon and fry until crispy, 10 to 15 minutes. Transfer bacon cubes to a plate, allow them to cool slightly and brush with the truffle honey. Reserve the pan.

FINISH SCALLOPS Heat butter and olive oil in a frying pan on high until very hot. Using tongs, gently place the scallops in the pan, reduce the heat to medium-high and cook on one side for about 3 minutes, until a crust forms on their bottoms and their tops are barely cooked. Transfer scallops to a plate.

Deglaze the pan with rhubarb sauce and set aside.

BREAD CRUMB TOPPING In the pan used to fry the bacon, melt butter on medium-high heat. Sprinkle in panko crumbs and thyme, stirring and cooking until they are buttery and toasty, 5 to 8 minutes.

TO ASSEMBLE Arrange a small pile of warm cabbage in the middle of 4 plates, top with 2 bacon cubes and arrange 3 scallops around the edge of each plate. Drizzle the scallops with the rhubarb glaze. Top with panko crumbs, dust with smoked paprika and serve immediately.

BREAD CRUMB TOPPING
¼ cup butter
2 cups panko crumbs
½ tsp fresh thyme leaves
Smoked paprika, for garnish

Lemon and Thyme-poached "Tuna in a Can"

SERVES 6 TO 8

A unique presentation of a delicious fish, "tuna in a can," or tuna conserva, packs a lot of flavour into a small mason jar. (You will need six to eight 1-cup mason jars for this recipe.) This dish, which involves poaching tuna in oil infused with lemon and thyme, has been on our menu from day one and will never come off it!

2 cups olive oil
1 ½ tsp kosher salt, plus more
    for seasoning
2 Tbsp finely diced shallots
2 lemons, in thin, round slices
4 sprigs fresh thyme
1 ¼ lb B.C. albacore tuna loins
12 to 16 toast points or crackers

In a tall, narrow pot large enough to hold the tuna, heat olive oil on medium to 70°F. (Use a deep-fat thermometer to test the temperature.) In a small bowl, combine salt, shallots, lemons and thyme, then add them to the pot. Using tongs, carefully submerge the tuna loins in the poaching oil. Cook for 1 ½ hours, checking regularly to ensure the oil is at 70°F (adjust the heat as needed).

Remove the pot from the heat and allow the tuna to cool in the oil for 30 minutes. Transfer the tuna to a baking sheet and refrigerate until cool, about 3 hours. Pour the poaching liquid (including the solids) into a bowl, cover and refrigerate until cool.

Using a slotted spoon, divide the tuna, shallots and herbs among the mason jars. Pour in enough poaching oil to just fill each jar and top with 1 lemon slice per serving. Chill before serving with toast points or crackers. Will keep refrigerated in an airtight container for up to 1 week.

Chicharrón with Tabasco and Lime

SERVES 4 TO 6

1 pork belly rind, about 5 lbs
¼ cup kosher salt
8 cups grapeseed oil,
  for deep frying
Dashes of Tabasco sauce
1 lime, in wedges

Crackled, crunchy and salty, fried pork rind—known to the Spanish as *chicharrón* and to the English as pork scratchings—is magical to all. The perfect appetizer or snack food, chicharrón is versatile and pairs as well with an off-dry Riesling as it does with cold beer and tequila. Begin this dish several hours before you plan to serve it.

Cut pork belly rind into strips about 6 inches long and 2 inches wide, making sure they are free of hair. Rinse thoroughly with cold water. Place strips in a large pot, add 1 Tbsp of the salt and fill the pot with enough water to just cover the meat. Bring the water to a simmer on medium-high. Simmer for 30 minutes, or until the strips feel tender when pressed between your fingers. Using tongs, remove the strips from the water, transfer them to a baking sheet and refrigerate for at least 3 hours.

With the back of a spoon, scrape the fat from the back of each cold pork strip and discard the fat. Sprinkle the strips generously with about 2 Tbsp of the salt and set aside for about 1 hour to draw some of the moisture out of the pork strip.

Preheat the oven to 170°F. Set a baking sheet on the lower rack. Pat the pork strips dry with paper towels, removing as much salt as possible. (Do not rinse off the salt using water.) Place the strips on the middle rack in the oven and bake for 1 ½ to 2 hours, until dehydrated and slightly crisp but still pliable. (Check on the rind regularly to make sure it doesn't burn.)

Preheat a deep fryer or half-fill a deep-sided pot with grapeseed oil and bring the temperature to 375°F. (Use a deep-fat thermometer to test the temperature.) Line a plate with paper towels. Cut the dehydrated pork strips into bite-sized pieces and fry until crisp, about 2 minutes. Using tongs or a slotted spoon, transfer chicharrón to the paper towel–lined plate and season immediately with the remaining 1 Tbsp salt. Just before serving, toss the crisps with some dashes of Tabasco and a squeeze or two of fresh lime juice.

Scallop Salad with Apples, Mangoes and Radishes

SERVES 4

LIME AND APPLE DRESSING

1 clove garlic

1 Granny Smith apple
   (or ⅓ cup good-quality
   apple juice)

Juice of ½ lime

¼ cup olive oil

1 tsp honey

SCALLOP SALAD

2 Tbsp olive oil

2 Tbsp wasabi oil

12 large scallops, thawed
   (if frozen)

Salt and black pepper

Juice of ½ lime

1 Granny Smith apple, peeled,
   cored and cut in ½-inch dice

1 mango, in ½-inch dice

5 radishes, thinly sliced

1 Tbsp microgreens

Pinches of Maldon salt, for garnish

Fresh and zingy, this colourful salad is easy to make. Serve it at lunch or as a starter with a loaf of crusty bread. The dressing is made by juicing an apple; however, feel free to use a good-quality apple juice instead. Wasabi oil can be bought at T & T or specialty food stores.

LIME AND APPLE DRESSING Using a handheld grater or a microplane, finely grate garlic. Place apple in a juicer and process until you have about ⅓ cup of juice. Discard the solids. In a glass jar with a lid, combine garlic, apple juice, lime juice, olive oil and honey. Shake until well blended and set aside.

SCALLOP SALAD In a small bowl, combine olive oil with wasabi oil. Using a very sharp knife, slice each scallop into 4 or 5 rounds. Arrange scallops in a clean bowl and season with salt, black pepper and lime juice. Pour the combined oils over the scallops and allow to marinate for at least 30 minutes and up to 1 hour.

TO ASSEMBLE Arrange a layer of apple and mango pieces either on individual plates or on a large serving platter. Top with the scallops, then a layer of radishes. Drizzle with the dressing and sprinkle with microgreens and Maldon salt. Serve immediately.

Braised Lamb Shanks with Ginger and Orange-glazed Carrots

SERVES 4

BRAISED LAMB SHANKS

4 Tbsp olive oil

4 carrots, in ½-inch dice

1 large Spanish onion or 2 small onions, in ½-inch dice

4 stalks celery, in ½-inch dice

4 lamb shanks

Salt

1 bulb garlic, minced

2 large tomatoes, quartered

1 sprig fresh thyme or rosemary, chopped

1 bay leaf

2 cups full-bodied red wine

4 cups chicken stock

GINGER AND ORANGE-GLAZED CARROTS

2 Tbsp grated fresh ginger

2 large carrots, peeled (or ½ cup good-quality carrot juice)

½ cup orange juice, preferably fresh-squeezed

12 baby carrots or multi-coloured heirloom carrots, if you can find them

⅓ cup butter, in 1-inch cubes (optional)

Lamb shanks are always a good idea, and they're especially excellent for a dinner party. Although this dish is easy to make, give yourself at least 5 hours, as the lamb needs time to cook and tenderize. Start the carrots about a half hour before you plan to serve the lamb— and purchase some good-quality carrot juice if you don't own a juicer.

BRAISED LAMB SHANKS Heat 2 Tbsp of the olive oil in a large sauté pan on medium-high until it is almost smoking. Stir in carrots, onions and celery and cook for about 20 minutes, until onions are translucent and celery and carrots are tender.

Coat the bottom of a large Dutch oven with the remaining 2 Tbsp olive oil and heat on high. Season lamb shanks with salt, place in the Dutch oven and sear on all sides until well browned, up to 25 minutes. Transfer the lamb shanks to a plate.

Preheat the oven to 375°F. Drain off and discard some of the fat from the Dutch oven and add carrots, onions, celery, garlic, tomatoes, thyme (or rosemary) and bay leaf. Reduce the heat to medium-high and cook for 5 more minutes, then deglaze the pan with the red wine and simmer for 20 to 30 minutes, until the liquid is reduced by ½. Return the lamb shanks to the Dutch oven and add the chicken stock. Cover and cook for 3 to 4 hours, or until the meat is so tender it is falling from the bones. Transfer the lamb shanks to a plate, cover loosely with aluminum foil and allow to rest for 30 minutes.

GINGER AND ORANGE-GLAZED CARROTS Place the ginger and large carrots in a juicer and process until you have ½ cup of juice. Discard the solids. (If using carrot juice, squeeze the grated ginger into the juice and discard the solids.) Pour the ginger-carrot juice into a medium saucepan, add orange juice and baby (or heirloom) carrots and cook on high heat until carrots are al dente, about 8 minutes. Using a slotted spoon, transfer the cooked carrots to a bowl and set aside. Continue cooking the sauce until reduced by ½, about 20 minutes. Set aside.

FINISH LAMB SHANKS Place a fine-mesh sieve over a small clean saucepan. Pour the braising liquid through the sieve, discarding any solids. Heat the braising liquid on high and cook for 15 to 20 minutes, until reduced by ½. Transfer to a serving bowl.

While the braising liquid is reducing, thicken the carrot-ginger sauce. Place it on medium-high heat and whisk in butter (if using) one cube at a time, until the sauce glistens and is emulsified. (You may not need all the butter cubes.) Return the cooked carrots to the sauce and warm through.

Arrange lamb shanks in a large serving dish, cover with the reduced braising liquid and serve with the ginger and orange–glazed carrots on the side. Serve hot.

SERVES 8

Chicken Fattee with Rice, Flatbread and Spiced Yogurt

ROAST CHICKEN

1 whole chicken, 2 to 3 lbs
Kosher salt
1 tsp ground allspice
2 Tbsp melted butter

TOMATO SAUCE

3 Tbsp olive oil
5 cloves garlic, minced
1 tsp ground allspice
2 cups passata (or
    crushed tomatoes)
Pinch of chili flakes
Salt

An elaborate multi-layered Lebanese dish, the fattee's different components can mostly be prepared ahead of time and assembled right before serving. It can easily feed more people by adding more layers. Passata is a simple purée of canned tomatoes; it has a light and fresh flavour and can be found in Italian grocery stores, where it's always sold in jars. (If you're feeling intrepid, you can make your own—see page 110.) When picking eggplants, make sure to get ones that are light in weight—they don't have as many seeds and are less bitter than the heavier ones.

ROAST CHICKEN Remove the chicken from the fridge, season it inside and out with salt and allspice, and allow it to rest, uncovered, on a plate at room temperature for 1 hour.

Preheat the oven to 450°F. Line a roasting pan just large enough to hold the chicken, with parchment paper. (The parchment paper prevents the skin from sticking to the pan.) Place chicken in the roasting pan and brush with melted butter. Roast for 20 minutes, breast side up. Using a pair of tongs, turn the chicken over—breast side down—and roast for another 20 minutes. Turn chicken over one more time (breast side up) and roast for a final 20 minutes. Transfer chicken to a clean cutting board, cover with aluminum foil and allow to cool. Deglaze the roasting pan with a splash of water, whisking to free the drippings stuck to the pan, then simmer the liquid for about 10 minutes to make a thick sauce.

When the chicken is cool enough to handle, use your hands and a fork to pull the meat off the bone into bite-sized pieces. Add chicken to the pan juices, toss well, then cover and set aside to keep warm.

TOMATO SAUCE Heat olive oil in a medium saucepan on medium. Add garlic and sauté until it starts to brown lightly, about 1 minute. Stir in allspice, followed by the passata and chili flakes to taste. Season the sauce with salt and simmer for 5 to 10 minutes. Set aside.

Continued overleaf…

CARAMELIZED ONIONS AND RICE

¼ cup butter

1 tsp ground allspice

1 onion, thinly sliced

2 cups basmati rice

3 cups chicken stock

Salt

FATTEE BASE AND TOPPINGS

1 cup Greek yogurt

1 clove garlic, minced

Salt

2 pita breads

2 Tbsp olive oil

1 Tbsp butter

¼ cup pine nuts

1 small bunch fresh Italian parsley, leaves only, roughly chopped

FRIED EGGPLANT

2 medium eggplants, unpeeled, in ½-inch dice

1 Tbsp kosher salt

¼ cup olive oil

CARAMELIZED ONIONS AND RICE Melt butter in a medium saucepan on medium. Stir in allspice and onions and sauté for 20 to 30 minutes, until golden and caramelized. Add rice and cook for 1 minute, stirring occasionally. Pour in chicken stock and season to taste with salt. Increase the heat to high, bring to a boil, then reduce the heat to low, cover and cook for 15 minutes. Turn off the heat and allow the rice to rest for 5 to 10 minutes.

FATTEE BASE AND TOPPINGS Preheat the oven to 400°F.

In a small bowl, combine yogurt with garlic. Season to taste with salt. Set aside.

Lightly brush pita bread with olive oil. Set on a baking sheet and cook until crisp, about 7 minutes. Transfer to a plate and set aside.

Melt butter in a small saucepan on medium-high heat. Add pine nuts and sauté for about 5 minutes, until golden. Set aside.

FRIED EGGPLANT Toss together eggplant and salt. Allow to rest for at least 30 minutes but no longer than an hour.

Line a plate with paper towels. To remove the salt from the eggplants, rinse under cold running water. Using your hands, squeeze excess moisture out of the eggplants. Allow to drain on the paper towel–lined plate.

Heat olive oil on medium-high, carefully add eggplant and sauté until golden and almost crispy, about 10 minutes. Using a slotted spoon, transfer eggplant to a bowl, cover and keep warm. Discard the oil.

TO ASSEMBLE Arrange pitas on a large serving platter. Cover completely with the rice, then top with the saucy roasted chicken. Sprinkle eggplant over the chicken, then drizzle with tomato sauce and yogurt-garlic mixture. Finish with parsley and pine nuts. Serve immediately.

Baked Eggs with Tomatoes, Peppers and Saffron

SERVES 6

Based on a Tunisian dish called *shakshuka,* these baked eggs are traditionally served for breakfast, but they make a perfect lunch dish paired with a simple green salad and lots of crusty bread for dipping. Look for the fiery hot Moroccan chili paste called *harissa* at specialty food stores, or substitute another chili paste.

Preheat the oven to 350°F. Place six 6-oz ramekins on a baking sheet.

Heat olive oil in a large sauté pan on medium. Add harissa, followed by bell peppers, garlic and cumin. Season generously with salt and cook for 10 to 15 minutes, or until peppers start to soften. Add tomatoes and the saffron mixture, bring the sauce to a gentle simmer and cook for 20 to 30 minutes, or until quite thick.

Divide the sauce among the ramekins. Using the back of a spoon, make a well in the centre of the sauce and crack an egg into it. Place the baking sheet in the oven and bake the eggs for 10 to 12 minutes. Rotate the baking sheet and cook for another 10 to 12 minutes, or until egg whites are just set and the yolks are still runny. Set the ramekins on individual plates, sprinkle with parsley and serve immediately.

¼ cup olive oil

3 Tbsp harissa paste

3 large red bell peppers, finely diced

4 cloves garlic, minced

1 tsp ground cumin

Kosher salt

5 large tomatoes, chopped

Pinch of saffron steeped in 2 Tbsp hot water

6 eggs

3 Tbsp roughly chopped parsley

CBLT (Coconut Bacon, Lettuce and Tomato) Sandwich

MAKES 4 SANDWICHES

Simple, toothsome and healthy, lunch has never been more delicious than this unique vegetarian CBLT.

CBLT SANDWICHES Preheat the oven to 300°F. In a glass baking dish, thoroughly combine coconut flakes, maple syrup, liquid smoke and tamari, ensuring that the flakes are completely coated. Bake, stirring the coconut every 7 to 10 minutes to make sure it doesn't burn, for about 25 minutes or until golden brown. Using a spoon, transfer coconut to a plate. Leave the oven on.

SPICY AIOLI Preheat the oven to 400°F. Place the shallot on a small baking sheet and brush generously with olive oil. Bake until soft and slightly charred, about 15 minutes. Remove from the oven and allow to cool, then peel shallot and trim off and discard the root end.

In a small food processor or a blender, blend roasted shallot, mayonnaise, mustard, paprika, chipotle pepper (if using), cider vinegar and salt to taste until well combined. Will keep refrigerated in an airtight container for up to 5 days.

TO ASSEMBLE Spread a generous amount of aioli on each slice of bread. Cover ½ of the bread slices with coconut, tomatoes, onions and lettuce. Cover with another slice of bread and serve immediately.

CBLT SANDWICHES

2 cups raw coconut ribbons (large flakes, if possible)
3 Tbsp maple syrup
1 ½ Tbsp liquid smoke
1 Tbsp tamari
1 loaf artisanal bread of your choice, in 8 slices
1 to 2 medium tomatoes, sliced
¼ red onion, thinly sliced
4 to 8 lettuce leaves

SPICY AIOLI

1 shallot
1 tsp olive oil
¼ cup + 2 Tbsp mayonnaise (we use Vegenaise)
2 Tbsp grainy mustard
1 Tbsp smoked paprika
½ tsp dried chipotle pepper (optional)
½ tsp apple cider vinegar
Salt

SERVES 4 TO 6

Roasted Garlic and White Bean Soup with Truffle Honey

4 bulbs garlic

Olive oil for drizzling

2 Tbsp butter

2 leeks, white part only, thinly sliced

2 tsp salt

¼ cup white wine

5 to 6 cups white beans, cooked

4 cups vegetable stock, plus more, if needed

1 can (13 oz) coconut milk, plus more, if needed

½ cup fresh lemon juice

¼ cup honey

¼ cup truffle oil

Salt and white pepper

18 sprigs fresh parsley, finely chopped, for garnish

Garlic and beans make a classic pairing. This hearty, healthy soup can be a starter or lunch. Serve on the side with the CBLT (page 61) for a more substantial meal.

Preheat oven to 375°F. Cut off the top ½ inch of each garlic bulb to expose the cloves. Drizzle generously with olive oil and wrap all 4 bulbs together in aluminum foil. Bake for about 1 hour, until garlic is soft and golden brown. Remove from the oven and set aside to cool.

While the garlic is roasting, melt butter in a large pot on medium heat. Add leeks and sauté until soft and translucent, about 10 minutes. Stir in salt and white wine and cook until reduced by ¾, about 3 minutes. Add white beans and vegetable stock, increase the heat to medium-high, and bring the mixture to a boil. Reduce the heat to medium and cook for 15 minutes.

Further reduce the heat to low and pour in the coconut milk and lemon juice. Squeeze the roasted garlic out of its skin and into the pot. Stir well to combine, then remove from the heat. Using a handheld blender, purée the soup until smooth. If it's thicker than you'd like, add more stock or coconut milk.

To make the truffle honey, combine honey and truffle oil in a squeeze bottle or a glass jar and shake until well blended.

To serve, season the soup to taste with salt and white pepper. Divide it equally among 4 to 6 bowls, drizzle with truffle honey and garnish with parsley.

Warm Chorizo and Frisée Salad

SERVES 4

Grilled chorizo with a soft-poached egg, pan-fried croutons and crumbled goat cheese on a bed of frisée tossed with a yuzu vinaigrette is the best brunch salad ever. Serve with a spicy Caesar cocktail. Yuzu juice is widely available at Japanese and Korean specialty food stores, but substitute equal parts orange and lemon juice, if you cannot find it.

YUZU VINAIGRETTE

¼ cup fresh yuzu juice

1 Tbsp dark, flavourful honey

1 tsp coriander seeds, toasted

1 Tbsp finely minced shallots

½ cup grapeseed oil

Salt and black pepper

CHORIZO AND FRISÉE SALAD

1 lb cured chorizo sausage

¼ cup olive oil

2 cups diced sourdough bread, in ½-inch cubes

Salt and black pepper

8 cups water

2 Tbsp white vinegar

4 eggs

2 heads frisée lettuce, leaves separated, washed and spun dry

1 ½ cups fresh goat cheese, crumbled (we use Fairwind Farms)

YUZU VINAIGRETTE In a small blender, mix yuzu juice, honey, coriander seeds and shallots on high speed for 1 minute. Reduce the speed to medium and slowly pour in the grapeseed oil until the vinaigrette is emulsified. Season with salt and black pepper. Will keep refrigerated in an airtight container for up to 1 week.

CHORIZO AND FRISÉE SALAD Preheat a grill or barbecue to medium-high. Using a sharp knife, slice chorizo in half lengthwise and then in half widthwise so that you have pieces that are 2 to 3 inches long. Grill the chorizo, turning the meat for 3 to 4 minutes, until it is covered in deep grill marks and hot all the way through. Set aside.

Line a plate with paper towels. In a medium sauté pan, heat olive oil on medium until it ripples. Carefully add bread cubes and cook, stirring constantly, until croutons are completely golden, 2 to 3 minutes. Using a slotted spoon, transfer the croutons to the paper towel–lined plate to drain. Season with a small amount of salt and black pepper. Set aside.

Line a plate with a tea towel. Combine the water and white vinegar in a heavy-bottomed pot and bring to a boil on high heat. Reduce the heat to medium-low or until the water is just simmering. Crack each egg into a small dish. Using a fork, stir the water in a clockwise direction to prevent the eggs from hitting and sticking to the bottom of the pot. Gently slide the eggs one at a time into the hot swirling water and cook for 4 minutes, until soft poached. Using a slotted spoon, carefully transfer the eggs to the tea towel–lined plate.

Place the frisée lettuce in a large salad bowl and toss with ½ of the vinaigrette. Sprinkle with the chorizo and top with the poached eggs and croutons. Drizzle with a bit more of the vinaigrette. Top with crumbled goat cheese, season with black pepper and serve immediately.

SERVES 4

Achiote-rubbed Boneless Chicken Thighs and Warm Hominy Salad

HOMINY SALAD

1 cup black beans, soaked overnight and drained

½ cup chopped red onions

¼ cup chopped fresh cilantro

1 Tbsp seeded, finely chopped jalapeño peppers

1 avocado, in ¼-inch dice

Juice of 2 limes

¼ cup olive oil

8 cups canola oil, for deep frying

2 cups dried hominy, soaked overnight and rinsed

Salt and black pepper

ACHIOTE-RUBBED CHICKEN THIGHS

1 poblano pepper

1 jalapeño pepper

1 red bell pepper

8 boneless chicken thighs, skin on

1 ½ cups diced cornbread or multigrain bread, in ¼-inch cubes

2 Tbsp chopped fresh cilantro

2 Tbsp achiote paste

1 Tbsp minced garlic

2 Tbsp extra-virgin olive oil

Salt and black pepper

1 tsp ground cumin, toasted

Quality ingredients are the key to any dish, but they'll make a big difference here. Look for naturally raised chicken thighs at good-quality butcher shops and farmers' markets. Buy fresh cornbread from your local bakery, and seek out the achiote paste and hominy from Latin and specialty food stores. Start this recipe a day in advance so that the black beans and hominy have time to soak for 24 hours (or buy them canned and add them directly to the onion-cilantro mixture, if you're pressed for time).

HOMINY SALAD Place black beans and enough fresh water to cover in a medium saucepan on medium-high heat. Simmer until tender, about 30 minutes, then drain them and transfer to a large bowl. Stir in onions, cilantro, jalapeños, avocado, lime juice and olive oil until well combined. Set aside at room temperature to allow the flavours to meld.

Preheat a deep fryer to 350°F or half-fill a large, deep pot with canola oil and bring it to 350°F on high heat. (Use a deep-fat thermometer to test the temperature, or drop a piece of hominy into the oil and if it sizzles quickly, it's ready.) Line a large plate with paper towels.

Using a fryer basket or a slotted spoon, lower hominy into the oil and cook until golden, about 5 minutes. Remove from the oil and transfer to the paper towel–lined plate to drain. Season to taste with salt and black pepper. Stir hominy into the bean mixture and season with more salt and black pepper as needed. Cover and refrigerate while you cook the chicken.

ACHIOTE-RUBBED CHICKEN THIGHS Preheat a barbecue to high. As soon as it's hot, place the poblano, jalapeño and red bell peppers on the grill and roast, turning them as they char, until their skin is blackened on all sides. Transfer to a large bowl, cover tightly with plastic wrap and set aside. Leave the barbecue on.

While the peppers are cooling, pat chicken thighs dry with paper towels. Set the chicken on a clean work surface and lightly pound them with a mallet to create a larger, flatter meat surface that will be easier to stuff and roll. Set aside.

Using a paring knife, peel and discard the blackened skin from the peppers. Remove and discard the seeds and stems, then dice peppers into ¼-inch cubes. In a bowl, toss peppers with cornbread (or multigrain bread) and cilantro. In a separate bowl, mix achiote paste with garlic and olive oil. Pour ½ of this spicy oil over the peppers and cornbread and fold in gently until the mixture is well coated and has the texture of a bread stuffing. (Reserve the rest of the spicy oil to rub onto the chicken.)

Cut 24 pieces of butcher's twine, each 10 inches long. Arrange chicken thighs skin side down on the work surface and season with salt and black pepper. Spoon 2 Tbsp of the stuffing into the middle of each chicken thigh. Fold one side of the chicken over the stuffing, then roll the chicken as tightly as possible into a log. Tie each roll at either end (about ½ inch from the end) and around the middle of the thigh. (This will ensure a consistent shape from end to end and will allow the chicken to cook more evenly.) Rub the stuffed, tied chicken thighs with the reserved spicy oil and sprinkle with cumin.

Place chicken on the barbecue and sear on all sides for about 5 minutes, or until a meat thermometer inserted in the thickest part of the thigh reads 160°F. Transfer cooked chicken to a plate, allow to cool slightly, then remove the twine and cut the thighs in half. Place two thighs on each plate and serve with the warm hominy salad.

Elk Lasagna

SERVES 10 TO 12

BOLOGNESE SAUCE

¼ cup olive oil

1 stalk celery, chopped

½ carrot, chopped

1 onion, chopped

2 lbs ground elk meat

2 Tbsp minced garlic

1 tsp finely chopped
fresh oregano

1 ½ cups red wine

4 cups canned tomatoes

CARAMELIZED ONIONS

¼ cup olive oil

2 Tbsp butter

2 lbs onions, julienned

Kosher salt

BÉCHAMEL SAUCE

4 cups whole milk

¼ onion, studded with
½ bay leaf and 2 cloves

¼ cup butter

¼ cup all-purpose flour

1 tsp dried thyme

Salt and black pepper

LASAGNA

1 cup grated parmesan

5 or more fresh pasta sheets

1 cup grated mozzarella

¼ cup chopped fresh
basil leaves or fresh
micro basil, for garnish

One of our most popular dishes at Cucina, this elk lasagna is more hearty and full-bodied than the traditional beef version. You can find elk at farmers' markets and at specialty butchers. You can also, of course, substitute beef. Make the sauce ahead of time, if you like. It will keep refrigerated in an airtight container for up to 1 week. Also, start the caramelized onions and the béchamel while the bolognese is cooking and cooling.

BOLOGNESE SAUCE Heat olive oil in a large pot on medium-high. Add celery, carrots and onions and cook until soft, about 10 minutes. Stir in elk meat, garlic and oregano and sauté for 2 minutes. When the meat is browned, add red wine and reduce until the liquid has evaporated, 10 to 15 minutes. Add the tomatoes, reduce the heat to low and simmer for 1 hour. Break up tomatoes with the back of a spoon, then set aside until completely cool.

CARAMELIZED ONIONS Heat olive oil and butter in a large pot on low. Add onions and a pinch of salt. (The salt will help draw more moisture out of the onions.) Cook, stirring the onions so that they don't stick to the bottom of the pan, until soft and dark brown but not burned, about 20 minutes. Remove from the heat and set aside to cool.

BÉCHAMEL SAUCE In a small pot, heat milk and studded onion on medium-high, until hot but not scalded, 8 to 10 minutes.

Melt butter in a large pot on medium-high heat. Gradually whisk in the flour and cook for about 5 minutes, until flour is absorbed. Remove and discard the onion from the hot milk, then slowly pour the milk into the flour mixture, whisking constantly to keep it smooth. Cook until the flour is incorporated and the sauce looks thick and creamy, about 8 minutes. Stir in thyme. (The béchamel needs to be very thick for the lasagna.) Season to taste with salt and black pepper.

LASAGNA Preheat the oven to 350°F. Ladle ¼ of the béchamel sauce into the bottom of a 10 x 12-inch baking dish. Sprinkle with ¼ of the parmesan, then top with ⅓ of the bolognese sauce and a single layer of pasta. Repeat with another ¼ of the béchamel sauce, ¼ of the parmesan and ⅓ of the bolognese sauce, followed by another layer of pasta. Completely cover the pasta with ¼ of the béchamel and then all of the caramelized onions. Top with another ¼ of the parmesan, the remaining ⅓ of the bolognese sauce and a final layer of pasta. Cover with the remaining ¼ of the béchamel sauce and the mozzarella. Bake for 1 hour, or until the cheese is golden. Just before serving, top with the remaining ¼ of the parmesan and garnish with basil. Bring to the table and serve!

Vitello Tonnato

SERVES 4

An elegant spin on surf and turf, veal (*vitello*) and tuna (*tonno*) served cold, is wonderful at brunch, as an appetizer, or at dinner with a salad, some olives and a glass of crisp Italian white wine.

Preheat the oven to 350°F. Heat olive oil in an ovenproof sauté pan on high until it's almost smoking. Season veal with a pinch of salt and black pepper and sear on all sides until brown, about 4 minutes. Transfer to the oven, cook for 5 minutes, then set aside until cool. Once cool, refrigerate veal for about 1 hour, or until completely cold. Using a very sharp knife, slice the veal as thinly as possible.

Place tuna, egg yolk, mustard and lemon juice in a food processor (or use a handheld mixer) and blend to combine. With the motor running, slowly pour in canola oil until the mixture has emulsified. When it is smooth, set aside.

Melt butter in a small sauté pan on medium heat until it starts to foam. Using a spoon, skim off the foam. Place a small fine-mesh sieve over a clean pot. Pour the butter through the sieve into the pot. Discard the solids, return the pot to the stove and add capers. Fry for about 5 minutes, until slightly crunchy, then set aside.

Brush a serving platter with a small amount olive oil. Arrange veal slices on top, then cover with the tuna emulsion. Garnish with fried capers, parsley and arugula. Season to taste with fleur de sel and black pepper.

1 Tbsp olive oil, plus more for brushing

½ lb milk-fed veal striploin

Salt and black pepper

1 can (7 oz) high-quality tuna packed in oil, drained

1 egg yolk

1 tsp Dijon mustard

Juice of ½ lemon

½ cup canola oil

1 Tbsp butter

¼ cup capers, drained

1 Tbsp fresh parsley leaves, for garnish

1 Tbsp chopped arugula, for garnish

Fleur de sel

CUISINE ET CHÂTEAU / THIERRY MERET AND MARNIE FUDGE

Goat's Milk Ricotta Cheesecake with Lemon and Rosemary

SERVES 8 TO 10 (MAKES ONE 9-INCH CAKE)

1 ½ cups finely ground graham cracker crumbs

1 cup + 6 Tbsp granulated sugar

6 Tbsp unsalted butter, room temperature

2 egg whites, room temperature

1 ¾ cups + 2 Tbsp fresh goat cheese, room temperature

1 ¼ cups goat's milk ricotta or regular ricotta

Zest of 2 lemons, finely grated

1 tsp finely chopped fresh rosemary

1 cup whipping cream

This delicious no-bake cheesecake is made with goat cheese, which brings a slightly nutty flavour to this dessert favourite. For a special occasion, garnish it with candied lemon zest. Buy candied peel or make your own by tossing fresh zest with a hot syrup made from equal parts of water and granulated sugar. Drain the zest, allow it to cool, then serve.

Preheat the oven to 375°F. Have ready a 9-inch springform pan.

In a large bowl, mix graham cracker crumbs, 5 Tbsp of the sugar and butter. Using your fingers, a knife or a pastry cutter, combine until the mixture resembles a coarse meal. Pour the crust mixture into the springform pan, pressing it flat, and bake for 8 minutes. Remove from the oven and allow it to cool completely.

While the crust is cooling, prepare the filling. In the top of a double boiler, combine ½ cup + 2 Tbsp sugar with the egg whites. Bring the water to a boil on high heat, then reduce to a simmer and heat the sugar and egg white mixture, stirring occasionally, until the sugar has dissolved. Remove from the heat. Using a whisk or a stand mixer, whisk the egg whites until they form stiff peaks. Set this meringue aside.

In a large bowl, combine goat cheese, ricotta, the remaining 7 Tbsp sugar, lemon zest and rosemary and mix until smooth.

Place the cream in the bowl of a stand mixer and whisk at medium-high speed until it forms soft peaks, 2 to 3 minutes. Using a spatula, gently fold the whipped cream into the cheese mixture. Next, carefully fold in the meringue. Pour the filling over the cooled crust. Refrigerate for at least 4 hours. Serve chilled.

Steamed Halibut en Papillote with Cranberry Mustard, Fennel and Goat Cheese

SERVES 6

CRANBERRY MUSTARD

2 Tbsp grainy mustard

1 Tbsp cranberry sauce

¼ tsp fresh lemon juice

STEAMED HALIBUT

¼ cup olive oil

2 small shallots, julienned

½ fennel bulb, cored and julienned

6 skinless, boneless
halibut steaks, each ¼ lb

1 small tomato, seeded
and cut in ½-inch dice

3 Tbsp fresh goat cheese, crumbled

Sea salt and black pepper

Roughly translated, the French word *papillote* means "wrapper," and this fish is steamed in a parchment paper wrapper, or pouch. Serving a dish *en papillote* makes for a wonderful presentation—a sort of food present arriving at the table. Opening up the hot parcel is a great conversation starter.

CRANBERRY MUSTARD In a small bowl, combine mustard, cranberry sauce and lemon juice until well mixed. Will keep refrigerated in an airtight container for up to 1 week.

STEAMED HALIBUT Preheat the oven to 400°F. Tear off 6 sheets of parchment paper, each 12 inches square. Cut each sheet into a teardrop shape. Arrange the sheets on a clean work surface with the pointed end toward you. Place 1 tsp of olive oil in the centre of each sheet. Divide the ingredients evenly among the 6 sheets: Place a layer of shallots on top of the oil. Follow with a layer of fennel, then top with a halibut steak. Add a layer of cranberry mustard, followed by layers of tomatoes, then goat cheese. Season each portion with salt and pepper. Drizzle another 1 tsp of olive oil over each portion.

To seal the packages, lift the left and right edges of the parchment paper toward each other (you may need to shift the layered ingredients to one side, then fold the other side of the paper over the filling). Starting at the pointed end, bring the edges of the paper together and fold them over to create a seal. Fold them a second time to prevent the seal from coming apart. Work your way toward the teardrop end of the paper, folding and folding again. To tighten the seal, lift the pointed end and tuck it underneath the papillote.

Arrange the parchment paper parcels (the papillotes) on a baking sheet and bake for 12 to 14 minutes, or until the papillote starts puffing. (As the parcel cooks, it starts to fill with steam, which cooks the fish.) Remove the parcels from the oven, slide them onto individual plates and very carefully cut open the top of each parcel with a pair of scissors (the escaping steam will be very, very hot) and serve immediately.

Seafood Ceviche

As with any seafood dish, it's really important to use fresh, sustainably sourced fish, particularly because ceviche is usually raw or only lightly "cooked." For best results, make the marinade a day in advance so that the flavours can really meld. Serve this dish with a chilled bottle of Prosecco.

MUSSELS Clean mussels, removing any beards adhering to the shells. Melt butter in a large sauté pan on medium-high until bubbling, then add garlic and jalapeño, stirring for about 1 minute, until garlic is soft. Stir in mussels and white wine and cook, covered, for 2 to 4 minutes, until the shells open. Remove from the heat, transfer the mussels to a bowl, and discard any mussels that haven't opened. Reserve 2 Tbsp of the cooking liquid in a small bowl.

Using a fork, remove the mussel meat from the shells and place it in a small bowl. Cover and refrigerate the mussel meat and the cooking liquid.

COCONUT-LIME DRESSING In a large bowl, whisk together lemon zest and juice, lime zest and juice, coconut milk, shallots, tomatoes, cilantro and aji amarillo paste (or Thai yellow curry paste) with the sugar and the reserved cooking liquid from the mussels. Season to taste with more lemon. Place a fine-mesh sieve over a small bowl. Pour the dressing through the sieve. Discard the solids. Set aside for at least 1 hour.

TUNA, SHRIMP AND SCALLOPS Fill a large bowl with ice water.

Season tuna with salt and black pepper. Heat canola oil in a large sauté pan on high, add tuna and sear for 10 seconds per side. Using tongs, plunge the tuna into the ice water for 20 seconds to stop the cooking. Dry the tuna with paper towels, then reserve it on a plate.

Continued overleaf…

MUSSELS

1 lb mussels

1 Tbsp unsalted butter, room temperature

1 clove garlic, minced

½ green jalapeño pepper, seeded and finely chopped

¼ cup dry white wine

COCONUT-LIME DRESSING

Zest and juice of 2 lemons

Zest and juice of ½ lime

¼ cup coconut milk

¼ cup roughly chopped shallots

½ medium tomato, roughly chopped

5 sprigs cilantro, minced

1 tsp aji amarillo paste (or Thai yellow curry paste)

1 tsp granulated or palm sugar

TUNA, SHRIMP AND SCALLOPS

¼ lb albacore tuna loin

Salt and black pepper

1 Tbsp canola oil

12 large shrimp, peeled

14 large scallops

Generous handful of microgreens, for garnish

Bring a large pot of salted water to a boil on high heat, then turn off the heat. When the water has stopped boiling, add shrimp and poach until they just start to turn pink, about 2 minutes. Using a slotted spoon, transfer the shrimp to the ice water to stop the cooking. Dry the shrimp with paper towels and set aside.

Using a very sharp knife, slice each scallop into 4 coin-sized medallions and set aside.

POPCORN GARNISH   On the stove or using a popcorn popper, pop popcorn kernels. Place the popcorn in a bowl. In a small bowl, combine butter, tandoori spice and salt to taste until well mixed, pour over the popcorn and toss lightly to coat.

TO ASSEMBLE   Arrange 5 mussels in a circle in the bottom of 4 individual bowls. Top with the scallops. Slice the shrimp in half lengthwise and arrange them over the scallops. Thinly slice the tuna and layer it on top of the shrimp.

Pour the dressing over the seafood, filling each bowl halfway. Garnish each serving with microgreens and popped corn, and serve immediately.

POPCORN GARNISH
2 Tbsp popcorn kernels
1 Tbsp melted unsalted butter
1 tsp tandoori spice
Salt

Lobster Broth

SERVES 4

1 whole live lobster, about 4 lbs
1 Tbsp olive or canola oil
½ cup diced carrots
½ cup diced onions
½ cup diced tomatoes
¼ cup fresh Thai basil leaves
2 cups whipping cream
Salt and black pepper
¼ cup butter
2 green onions, finely chopped
Paprika, for garnish

A creamy, savoury soup that's perfect for an elegant afternoon brunch or served in small bowls as an amuse-bouche for a larger party. Serve it with a bottle of white Burgundy. We recommend that you buy a live lobster and kill it just before cooking (do this humanely by driving a knife through the base of its head); if you're not comfortable doing this, have your fishmonger separate the lobster into body, claws and tail.

Fill a very large bowl with ice water. Bring a large pot of salted water to a boil on high heat. Place the live lobster in the sink, using tongs to hold it steady with one hand. Quickly sink a very sharp knife into the flesh at the base of the head to kill the lobster, then separate the into the body, tail and claws.

Add all the lobster pieces except the little claws to the boiling water and cook for 4 minutes each. Using tongs, transfer the cooked lobster to the ice bath for 1 minute to stop the cooking. Boil the claws for 3 minutes, then plunge them in the ice water for 1 minute. Transfer the cooled lobster to a plate. Reserve 4 cups of the cooking water and discard the rest.

Using a nutcracker and a fork, remove the lobster meat from the shells (discard the shells or freeze them to make stock for another recipe). Set aside the meat from the tail and claws. Chop the meat from the lobster body into bite-sized chunks.

Heat olive (or canola) oil in a large saucepan on high. Add the chunks of lobster body and sear until they turn red, 2 to 3 minutes. Stir in carrots and onions and cook until tender but not browned, about 5 minutes. Add tomatoes, Thai basil and the reserved lobster water and bring to a boil. Reduce the heat to medium, skim off any foam at the surface and simmer for 1 hour.

Place a fine-mesh sieve over a clean pot. Pour the boiled lobster and stock through the sieve. Reserve the stock, but discard the solids. Place the pot on high heat and boil until the stock is reduced by ½, 20 to 30 minutes.

Heat cream in a medium saucepan on medium-high and cook until reduced by ½, about 15 minutes. Add the reduced lobster stock and season to taste with salt and black pepper. Set aside.

Melt butter in a saucepan on medium heat. Add the meat from the lobster tails and claws and cook until heated through, about 5 minutes. Divide the lobster among 4 individual soup bowls and sprinkle with green onions.

Place the cream and lobster stock in a blender or food processor, and blend on high until light and frothy. Pour this mixture over the lobster and green onions. Dust with paprika and serve hot.

Janice's Bubbling Mac 'n' Cheese

**SERVES 4 AS A MAIN COURSE
OR 6 AS A SIDE**

5 ¼ cups penne
6 cups whole milk
⅓ cup unsalted butter
¾ cup finely diced onions
1 ½ Tbsp minced garlic
½ cup all-purpose flour
⅓ cup Dijon mustard
¼ tsp cayenne pepper
Sea salt and black pepper
2 ½ cups grated 3-year-old
    white cheddar
2 ½ cups grated Gruyère
1 cup dry bread crumbs

We serve this signature dish in its own casserole with a side of house-made pickles. Bubbling hot macaroni 'n' cheese is the queen of comfort foods, and the addition of a little cayenne gives a smooth, subtle heat to the abundant cheesy goodness. Serve with a tart green salad, chunks of fresh bread and a red or white wine from France's Jura or Savoie regions. Embrace the cheese!

Preheat the oven to 400°F. Bring a large pot of salted water to a boil on high heat. Add penne and cook according to the package directions until just al dente. Drain the pasta and set aside.

While the pasta is cooking, heat milk in a small saucepan on medium. In another saucepan, melt butter on medium heat. Add onions and garlic and sauté 5 to 10 minutes, or until onions are translucent. Stir in flour for 2 to 3 minutes or until it forms a thick paste (a roux). Slowly add hot milk, mustard and cayenne, whisking constantly. Season to taste with salt and black pepper. Stirring occasionally, cook this béchamel sauce for 10 minutes, or until creamy and smooth. Add the cheeses, stirring until melted and incorporated. Adjust the seasoning, as necessary.

In a shallow casserole dish or a Dutch oven, combine béchamel sauce and cooked penne until well mixed. Top with bread crumbs. (At this point, you can freeze the mac 'n' cheese in an airtight container for future use. Bring it to room temperature before baking it.) Cover the pan with aluminum foil and bake for 15 minutes, or until bubbly and golden around the edges. Remove the foil and bake for another 15 minutes, or until the bread crumbs turn golden. Serve immediately.

SERVES 4

Goat Cheese Fritter Salad with Apples and Toasted Almonds

HONEY-MUSTARD VINAIGRETTE

2 Tbsp champagne or sherry vinegar

1 Tbsp grainy mustard (we use brassica mustard)

1 Tbsp mild honey (we use Chinook honey)

½ cup olive oil

Sea salt and black pepper

GOAT CHEESE SALAD

½ cup all-purpose flour

Sea salt and black pepper

1 egg, lightly beaten

1 cup panko or dry bread crumbs

4 slices of firm goat cheese, each ¼ inch thick

1 tsp olive oil

1 tsp butter

8 cups salad greens (we use Hotchkiss organic)

1 medium sweet onion, sliced and sautéed in butter

1 apple, such as Fuji or Ambrosia, cored and thinly sliced

¼ cup almonds, toasted and roughly chopped

We make this salad using a firm goat cheese log, such as Paillot de Chèvre, and we also have the fritters prepared in the shop, ready for you to take home if you are pressed for time. Depending on the season, you can substitute roasted beets or grapefruit for the apples in this salad.

HONEY-MUSTARD VINAIGRETTE In a large glass jar, combine champagne (or sherry) vinegar, mustard, honey and olive oil. Shake well until emulsified, then season to taste with salt and black pepper. Will keep refrigerated in an airtight container for up to 1 week.

GOAT CHEESE SALAD Place flour on a plate and season it with a pinch of salt and a generous grinding of black pepper. Pour egg into a large shallow bowl. Arrange panko crumbs (or dry bread crumbs) on a second plate. Dredge cheese slices first in flour, then egg, then panko (or bread) crumbs. Set aside.

In a frying pan on medium-high, heat olive oil and butter. Add the breaded cheese slices and cook on both sides until crispy and golden and the cheese is oozing a bit, about 5 minutes total. Remove from the heat.

In a large bowl, toss the greens with the vinaigrette until well coated. Mound the greens on 4 plates. Top with onions, apples and toasted almonds and add one cheese fritter per person. Season to taste with salt and black pepper. Serve immediately.

Radicchio Salad with Poached Pears and Burrata

SERVES 6 TO 8

4 Anjou pears, firm to the touch

1 ¾ cups white wine

1 sprig fresh thyme

¾ cup granulated sugar

2 tsp Dijon mustard

3 Tbsp white balsamic vinegar

¾ cup canola oil

4 heads radicchio, cut in quarters

3 whole burrata, broken into pieces (we prefer White Gold's cheese)

Olive oil for drizzling

Truffle oil for drizzling

Salt

1 ⅔ cups whole blanched almonds, toasted (optional)

Buffalo mozzarella is delicious, but burrata is its even tastier, creamier cousin. Burrata's centre has been enriched with cream, and the combination of the rich burrata and sweet pears perfectly balances the bitter radicchio. Serve this salad as a side dish with pork or on its own for lunch.

Peel pears, cut them in half and core them. Combine white wine, thyme and ¼ cup of the sugar in a large pot and add pears, making sure they are submerged. Bring the pot to a boil on medium-high, then reduce the heat to medium-low and simmer for about 10 minutes or until pears are easily pierced with a fork. Using a slotted spoon, transfer poached pears to a bowl.

Pour the poaching liquid into a small saucepan, add the remaining ½ cup sugar and cook on medium heat until reduced by ¾, about 5 minutes. (You should have ½ cup.)

Pour the reduced syrup into a blender. Add mustard and balsamic vinegar and process on medium speed until well combined. With the motor running, slowly add canola oil until the vinaigrette is emulsified. Set aside.

Place radicchio in a large bowl, add vinaigrette and toss until well coated. Divide the radicchio among individual plates. Cut pears into thin slices and arrange over the radicchio, then top with a chunk of burrata. Drizzle each serving lightly with olive oil and truffle oil, then sprinkle with salt to taste. Top with almonds and serve immediately.

Leek and Mushroom Portafoglio

SERVES 8 TO 10

LEEK AND MUSHROOM PORTAFOGLIO

4 cups all-purpose flour, plus more, if needed

15 egg yolks

4 leeks, white parts only

¼ cup unsalted butter

2 lbs mushrooms, stems removed and thinly sliced (we use half cremini and half portobello)

3 sprigs fresh thyme, leaves only

3 Tbsp mascarpone

2 eggs

Salt and black pepper

In Italian, *portafoglio* means "wallet," which is a good description for this pasta filled with a delicious leek and mushroom filling. While ravioli is usually two sheets of pasta with a filling sandwiched between, portafoglio is one sheet of pasta rolled around the filling. If you have a pasta machine, roll out the pasta dough yourself and feed your friends a fantastic dinner of homemade egg noodles, or buy fresh pre-made pasta from an Italian market. Serve with a side of Radicchio Salad with Poached Pears and Burrata (page 84).

This pasta freezes well: make a batch, arrange the individual pasta on a baking sheet and freeze them, then pop the portafoglio in a resealable plastic bag and store them in the freezer for 6 to 8 weeks.

To serve, simply cook them from frozen.

LEEK AND MUSHROOM PORTAFOGLIO Mound the flour on a clean work surface and make a well in the middle. Add egg yolks all at once and, using your hands, slowly start to incorporate the flour into the yolks, working from the inside of the well out. Form the mixture into a ball and knead until smooth but not sticky. (Add more flour as required to make a firm dough.) Wrap dough in plastic wrap and refrigerate for at least 30 minutes.

While the pasta dough is resting, make the filling. Cut leeks in half and rinse under cold water to remove any sand. Cut the halves into ½-inch-thick semi-circles. Melt 2 Tbsp of the butter in a sauté pan on medium heat, add leeks and cook until translucent, about 8 minutes. In a second sauté pan, melt the remaining 2 Tbsp butter on medium heat, add mushrooms and cook until browned, about 4 minutes. Stir leeks into the mushrooms, fold in thyme, mascarpone and whole eggs and season with salt and black pepper. Set aside.

Cut pasta dough into 8 equal portions. Cover the portions you're not using while you roll out the rest of the pasta. (For best results, roll 2 portions of the pasta and fill them, then roll out the next 2 and fill them, repeating until you have rolled and filled all the pasta.) Using a pasta machine, roll one portion at a time, starting at the thickest and rolling it through progressively thinner settings until you reach the second-to-last setting or about 1 mm thick. You should have large sheets of really thin, delicate pasta, each about 3 inches wide by 20 inches long.

To fill the pasta, arrange a sheet of pasta on a clean work surface, with the long side parallel to the edge of the counter. Using a spoon, drop about ½ Tbsp of the leek and mushroom filling onto the bottom left-hand corner of the sheet, placing it about 1 inch away from the edges. Repeat with the remaining filling, arranging the mounds in a single row and leaving ½ inch between each one. Lightly brush the pasta around the filling with water, then fold the 1-inch-wide bottom edge over the filling, pressing the dough around the mounds to form a tightly contained pocket. Using a pasta wheel, cut the pasta into individual squares. Repeat with the remaining pasta and filling. You should have about 60 squares in total.

GARLIC CREAM SAUCE   Melt butter in a saucepan on medium heat. Add shallots and garlic and sauté until soft and just starting to brown, about 2 minutes. Deglaze the pan with the white wine and reduce until almost dry, about 2 minutes. Stir in cream and reduce by ⅓, about 6 minutes, then add mascarpone.

FINISH PORTAFOGLIO   Bring a large pot of heavily salted water to a boil on high heat. Add pasta and cook for 5 to 6 minutes, until al dente. Drain immediately and mix the cream sauce into the drained pasta and warm it through. Serve warm.

GARLIC CREAM SAUCE
1 Tbsp butter
2 tsp finely diced shallots
2 tsp minced garlic
¼ cup white wine
2 ¼ cups whipping cream
5 Tbsp mascarpone

Strawberry Shortcake Doughnuts

**SERVES 6 TO 8
(MAKES 16 TO 18 DOUGHNUTS)**

Nothing is more delicious than a freshly made doughnut filled with strawberries and cream—really, nothing! Try this recipe for a birthday celebration or a dinner party, accompanied by strong coffee or small glasses of Moscato.

CAKE DOUGHNUTS In a medium bowl, combine flour, baking soda and salt and set aside. In a second medium bowl, combine sour cream and buttermilk until well mixed and set aside.

Place egg and sugar in the bowl of a stand mixer fitted with a paddle attachment and beat on high speed until thoroughly combined. Add butter and beat until well mixed. Pour in ½ of the flour mixture and beat until incorporated. Add the sour cream–buttermilk combination and beat until well mixed. Pour in the remaining flour mixture and beat until a stiff batter forms.

Half-fill a deep-sided pot with peanut (or other) oil and heat to 375°F. (Use a deep-fat thermometer to check the temperature. Alternatively, drop a pinch of the batter into the oil and if it sizzles rapidly, it's ready.) Wet your hands, then scoop out ¼ cup batter, roll it into a ball and flatten it slightly. Set the doughnut on a baking sheet. Repeat with the remaining batter, keeping your hands wet to prevent the dough from sticking, until you have 16 to 18 doughnuts.

Line a plate with paper towels. Using a slotted spoon, carefully drop the doughnuts into the hot oil, a few at a time, and cook until they are golden and float to the top, about 3 minutes each. Transfer to the paper towel-lined plate to drain. Allow them to cool, then cut them in half horizontally. Set aside.

CREAM FILLING Using a stand mixer fitted with a whisk, whip cream on medium until soft peaks form, about 8 minutes. Add icing sugar and vanilla and beat until stiff, about 5 minutes.

TO ASSEMBLE Scoop the cream filling into a piping bag fitted with a ¼-inch plain tip and pipe a generous amount of filling onto the bottom ½ of each doughnut. Top with strawberries, cover with the top ½ of the doughnut and dust with icing sugar. Serve immediately.

CAKE DOUGHNUTS

4 ½ cups all-purpose flour

1 ½ tsp baking soda

½ tsp salt

¼ cup sour cream

1 cup buttermilk

1 egg, room temperature

1 cup + 2 Tbsp granulated sugar

2 ½ Tbsp melted unsalted butter

4 cups peanut, grapeseed or canola oil, for deep frying

2 cups sliced fresh strawberries

CREAM FILLING

2 cups whipping cream

¼ cup icing sugar, plus more for garnish

¼ tsp vanilla extract

Sticky Toffee Doughnuts

SERVES 12

DOUGHNUT BATTER

2 ¾ cups cake flour, plus
  more for dusting

1 tsp baking powder

1 tsp salt

½ cup pitted dates, chopped

⅔ cup granulated sugar

2 Tbsp shortening

⅔ cup whole milk, room
  temperature

1 egg, room temperature

1 egg yolk, room temperature

2 lbs solid shortening, for
  deep frying

WHIPPED CARAMEL CREAM

1 cup whipping cream

¼ cup dark brown sugar

STICKY TOFFEE SYRUP

2 cups dark brown sugar

⅔ cup water

1 cup (½ lb) unsalted butter

Hot, fresh doughnuts are a thing of beauty, and this straightforward, simple recipe will impress your friends and make you look like a professional baker. Start the dough a day before and leave it in the fridge overnight, or simply allow it to rest for an hour.

DOUGHNUT BATTER Sift the flour, baking powder and salt into a bowl, then add the dates and toss well. In the bowl of a stand mixer fitted with a paddle attachment, cream the sugar and the shortening for 1 minute on medium-high speed. Beat in the milk, egg and egg yolk and continue to beat for 1 minute more, until the mixture is pale and fluffy. Reduce the speed to low, then add the dry ingredients in 3 parts, scraping down the sides of the bowl after each addition. The resulting dough will be sticky, not unlike a very wet cookie dough or biscuit. Transfer the dough to a clean bowl, cover and refrigerate for 1 hour or overnight.

WHIPPED CARAMEL CREAM Refrigerate the bowl from a stand mixer until chilled. Place the cream in the bowl of the stand mixer and whip until it forms soft peaks, about 5 minutes. Add brown sugar and continue to whip until very stiff, about 10 minutes. Scrape the mixture into a clean bowl, cover and refrigerate until required, but no longer than 30 minutes, to prevent a skin from forming on the cream.

STICKY TOFFEE SYRUP Place the brown sugar, water and butter in a heavy-bottomed saucepan and bring to a boil on medium heat. Boil until the syrup is slightly thickened, about 20 minutes. Remove from the heat and use immediately.

FINISH DOUGHNUTS Lightly dust a clean work surface with cake flour. Dust the top of the dough and a rolling pin to prevent sticking, then gently roll out the dough to a circle about 8 inches in diameter and ½ inch thick. Dust a 3-inch round doughnut cutter with flour, then cut out as many doughnuts and holes as possible, gently folding and rerolling the scraps to make about 12 doughnuts.

Line a plate with paper towels. Melt the shortening in a large, deep-sided pot on high heat until it reaches 370°F. (Use a deep-fat thermometer to test the temperature.) Gently shake off as much of the excess flour from the doughnuts as possible, then, using a slotted spoon, carefully slide them, one at a time, onto the surface of the hot oil, being careful not to splatter the oil. Fry 3 doughnuts at a time so that you don't lower the temperature of the oil. Cook for 1 minute, then flip them once and cook for another minute. Transfer to the paper towel–lined plate to drain and allow to cool for 1 minute.

Place the warm doughnuts on a baking sheet and carefully brush them with the warm syrup, repeating the glazing until all the syrup is used. Allow to cool to room temperature (do not refrigerate).

Scrape the whipped cream into a piping bag fitted with a star tip, pipe stars or rosettes on the doughnuts and serve immediately.

Mike's Drunken Spanish Toast Recipe

SERVES 4 HUNGRY PEOPLE, 6 NOT SO HUNGRY

1 ½ bottles (750 mL + 375 mL) full-bodied red wine

2 cinnamon sticks

1 vanilla bean, split lengthwise

1 cup granulated sugar

½ cup water

½ cup honey

4 sprigs fresh thyme

1 loaf dense, day-old artisanal bread

1 cup all-purpose flour

4 eggs

⅛ cup whole milk

2 Tbsp butter

2 Tbsp canola oil

Salted caramel ice cream (optional)

The Spanish have been generous enough to share their recipe for bread marinated in red wine syrup, rolled in egg, fried and finished with thyme-infused honey. This version comes from Mike Wrinch, the general manager of Knifewear Calgary and a former chef with some serious chops. Make sure to buy a dense loaf of artisanal bread a day ahead so that it will hold together.

Combine red wine, cinnamon sticks, vanilla and sugar in a medium saucepan and simmer on medium heat until reduced by ⅓, about 15 minutes. Remove from the heat and allow to cool.

In a small saucepan, bring water and honey to a simmer on medium heat. Cook for about 5 minutes, add thyme and allow to steep for 5 minutes. Set aside.

Cut bread into 2-inch cubes, then add to red wine syrup and allow to absorb the liquid for 2 minutes.

Line a plate with paper towels. Place flour in a shallow bowl. Crack eggs into a second bowl, add milk and whisk until well combined. Melt butter and canola oil in a frying pan on medium heat. Using your hands, squeeze excess wine syrup from one of the bread cubes. Dredge the bread in flour, shake off the excess and then dip it in the egg mixture and roll it around. Repeat with all remaining bread cubes. Place the bread cubes in the frying pan in batches, and cook them on all sides until slightly crispy (we'd say golden, but the bread is pink from the marinade!), about 5 minutes. Transfer the bread to the paper towel–lined plate.

Heap the fried bread on a serving platter and drizzle with thyme syrup. For added decadence, serve with salted caramel ice cream.

Gin and Tonic Jelly with Pimm's No. 1 Cup Salad

SERVES 6

GIN AND TONIC JELLY

1 ¼ cups + 2 Tbsp water

1 ¼ cups granulated sugar

Zest and juice of 2 limes

1 ¾ cups tonic water

1 cup gin

1 ½ Tbsp powdered gelatin

PIMM'S SALAD

1 Gala or Honeycrisp apple, peeled, cored and sliced

1 orange, in segments

8 fresh strawberries, sliced

2-inch piece of English cucumber, julienned

5 fresh mint leaves, in chiffonade

2 Tbsp Pimm's

¼ to ½ cup whipped cream

6 good-quality shortbread cookies, for garnish

Summer makes me think of pitchers of Pimm's in the garden. The best Pimm's pitcher has so much fruit (apple, cucumber, strawberry, orange, plus mint) that it borders on a salad. To go the bonus round on a hot afternoon, add a splash of gin with your ginger ale or make this Pimm's Cup Salad instead. Start the jelly in the morning to give it time to set. Ya gotta love the summer.

GIN AND TONIC JELLY Arrange 6 tumblers on a baking sheet. In a medium pot, bring 1 ¼ cups of the water and sugar to a boil on high heat until sugar dissolves. Remove it from the heat and add the lime zest. Allow to steep for 10 minutes.

Place a fine-mesh sieve over a large measuring cup and pour the infused syrup into the sieve. Discard the solids. Add lime juice, tonic and gin. (You should have about 3 cups of liquid. If you're a bit short, add more gin, tonic or lime juice, according to your taste.)

Measure 2 Tbsp cold water into a small bowl, then add gelatin powder and allow it to bloom for 5 minutes. Add ¼ cup of the gin mixture to the gelatin, then tip the gelatin into the measuring cup. Pour the jelly mixture into the tumblers and refrigerate until set, about 6 hours.

PIMM'S SALAD Combine apples, oranges, strawberries, cucumbers and mint in a glass salad bowl. Pour in Pimm's and allow the fruit to macerate for 10 to 15 minutes.

To serve, top the jelly in the tumblers with fruit salad, add a dab of whipped cream and garnish with a shortbread cookie.

Black Truffle and White Cheddar Fondue

SERVES 2 TO 3

Fondue is always a good idea because there's nothing cozier than sharing a pot of hot, bubbling cheese with friends. Among our favourite foods to dip in this fondue are cubes of cooked tenderloin, Italian sausage, prosciutto, grilled chicken, prawns, lobster, apples, asparagus, broccolini, potatoes… the list is endless.

In a small bowl, combine cheddar and parmesan cheeses and set aside.

Combine white wine, chicken stock, garlic and chili oils, truffles, salt and white pepper in a medium saucepan and bring to a boil on medium-high heat. Reduce the heat to low and stir in mixed cheeses.

In a small bowl, mix cornstarch and water until fully dissolved. Slowly add the cornstarch mixture to the melted cheeses, stirring constantly until the fondue thickens. Season to taste with salt and white pepper.

Set a cast-iron fondue pot over a low flame. Pour the cheese mixture into the fondue pot and stir in truffle oil to taste. Arrange bread, meats and/or boiled vegetables in separate bowls, pass around the fondue forks and dig in.

1 cup grated aged white cheddar

1 cup grated parmesan

½ cup dry white wine, not sweet

¼ cup chicken stock

1 Tbsp garlic oil (page 97)

1 Tbsp chili oil (page 97)

1 tsp truffle peelings

Salt and white pepper

2 Tbsp cornstarch

2 Tbsp cold water

Black truffle oil, for drizzling

A loaf of your favourite bread cut in cubes, cooked meats and/or boiled root vegetables, asparagus or broccolini, for dipping

Beef Tartare

SERVES 6 TO 8

Beef tartare is a classic dish that you can make your own by person-alizing the ingredients you choose. Silky, rich and satisfying, it has a wonderful mouth feel and umami flavour. The beef in this recipe is raw, so buy the freshest, best-quality meat you can and use scrupu-lously clean knives, boards and bowls while you prepare it. Use the leftover oil from this dish to fry or garnish grilled meats or fish.

CHILI OIL In a small saucepan, combine canola oil, chili flakes and paprika on low heat and cook for 30 minutes. Remove from the heat and allow to steep for another 30 minutes. Place a paper coffee filter over a small bowl. Strain the oil through the filter and discard the chili flakes. Set aside the oil.

GARLIC OIL In a small saucepan on medium heat, simmer olive (or canola) oil and garlic for about 10 minutes, until garlic is light brown and lightly roasted. Place a paper coffee filter over a small bowl. Strain the oil through the filter and discard the garlic. Set aside the oil.

BEEF TARTARE Using a very sharp knife, coarsely chop the beef. (Do not use a food processor, as it gives the tartare an unpleasant, ground beef–like texture.) In a small bowl, combine chili and garlic oils. Whisk in egg yolks and black pepper. Add to the chopped meat, mixing well. Stir in gherkins, mustard, shallots, capers and fleur de sel. Adjust the seasonings, as needed. Arrange the tartare in a serving bowl, cover tightly with plastic wrap and refrigerate until well chilled.

Remove from the fridge and serve immediately with potato chips, toast points, rice crackers or bread.

CHILI OIL
1 cup canola oil
¼ cup chili flakes
2 Tbsp paprika

GARLIC OIL
1 cup mild-tasting olive oil
    or canola oil
8 cloves garlic

BEEF TARTARE
1 lb beef tenderloin,
    trimmed of fat
2 Tbsp chili oil
2 Tbsp garlic oil
2 egg yolks
2 tsp black pepper
10 gherkins, finely minced
2 Tbsp Dijon mustard
2 Tbsp finely minced shallots
2 Tbsp capers, drained
2 Tbsp fleur de sel
12 to 16 potato chips,
    toast points, rice crackers
    or slices of bread

B.C. Albacore Crudo

SERVES 4 AS AN APPETIZER

GREEN ONION KIMCHEE

2 cloves garlic

2-inch knob fresh ginger

1 cup fish sauce

1 Tbsp granulated sugar

1 tsp kosher salt

2 Tbsp gochujang (Korean red pepper paste)

2 lbs green onions, green parts only, roughly chopped

BURNT SHALLOT AIOLI

6 medium shallots, peeled and halved

2 Tbsp olive oil

2 whole eggs

1 tsp Dijon mustard

½ cup canola oil (we prefer Highwood Crossing)

Salt

Italy and Asia share many similarities in their cuisines, including a love of noodles, rice and fresh fish. Crudo has been described as "sashimi with an Italian soul." Use the highest-quality albacore tuna you can find and ask your fishmonger to slice it for you. Homemade kimchee is well worth the effort; however, if you are unable to make your own (or if you're in a hurry and don't want to wait 5 days!), substitute a quality store-bought kimchee, which is available at all Asian markets. Three Farmers Camelina oil is produced in Saskatchewan; it has an admirable nutritional profile and has a unique fruity, earthy flavour that is worth seeking out.

GREEN ONION KIMCHEE Place garlic, ginger, fish sauce, sugar, salt and gochujang in a blender and purée until smooth. Place green onions into a large resealable plastic bag, add the paste and toss together until well mixed. Allow the green onions to ferment at room temperature for 5 days. (The bag will start to expand and that's a good thing—just release some of the air to prevent a kimchee explosion!) After 5 days, release all of the air from the bag and refrigerate for up to 4 weeks.

BURNT SHALLOT AIOLI Preheat the oven to 400°F. Place shallots on a baking sheet and toss with the olive oil until well coated. Roast until well browned and caramelized all over, 15 to 20 minutes. Remove from the oven and allow to cool. (You can also grill rather than roast the shallots.)

Bring a medium pot of water to a boil on high heat. Add eggs and cook for 2 minutes. Remove from the heat, and place under cold running water to stop the cooking. Crack the eggs and scoop out whites and yolks into a blender. Add shallots and mustard and pulse until well mixed. With the motor running, slowly drizzle the canola oil into the mixture until it emulsifies to the consistency of mayonnaise (you may not need all of the oil). Season to taste with salt. Will keep refrigerated in an airtight container for up to 1 week.

PICKLED SHALLOTS Place cinnamon stick, peppercorns and star anise in the middle of a square piece of cheesecloth, gather up the edges and tie them together with butcher's twine to make a bouquet garni.

Bring red wine vinegar and water to a boil in a large pot on high heat. Add sugar and bouquet garni, then stir in shallots and boil for 3 minutes. Using a slotted spoon, transfer shallots to a bowl and allow to cool to room temperature, about 15 minutes. Keep the pickling liquid boiling to reduce slightly, and when the shallots are cool, boil them for another 3 minutes. The shallots will be iridescent, tender and pink. Drain shallots and discard the pickling liquid and the bouquet garni. Boiling the onions twice creates a vibrant colour and al dente texture.

GARLIC CHIPS Place milk in a small pot, add garlic and scald on medium-high heat for 15 minutes. Do not allow the milk to boil. Using a slotted spoon, transfer garlic to a plate and pat dry with paper towels. Discard the milk.

Line a plate with paper towels. Heat canola oil in a medium frying pan on high until hot, then add garlic and fry until golden and crispy, about 1 minute (do not overcook, as they can become bitter). Using a slotted spoon, transfer to the paper towel–lined plate. Set aside.

CRUDO Arrange tuna in a line in the centre of a serving platter and season with a sprinkle of Maldon salt and a drizzle of camelina oil. Around the tuna, set individual mounds of green onion kimchee, pickled shallots, garlic chips, trout roe, nasturtium leaves and drizzle with burnt shallot aioli. Add a squeeze of lemon juice and a sprinkle of Maldon salt. Top with micro herbs.

PICKLED SHALLOTS

1 cinnamon stick

1 tsp black peppercorns

1 pod star anise

4 cups red wine vinegar

2 cups water

1 cup granulated sugar

20 shallots, peeled and sliced

GARLIC CHIPS

½ cup whole milk

8 cloves garlic, thickly sliced

2 cups canola oil for frying

CRUDO

5 oz albacore tuna loin, in ½-inch slices

Maldon salt

Camelina oil (or cold-pressed canola oil), for garnish

1 tsp cured trout roe, for garnish

3 small nasturtium leaves, for garnish

1 lemon, in wedges, for garnish

Micro herbs, for garnish

Mo-lacquered Pork Belly and Seared Scallops

SERVES 8

BRAISED PORK BELLY

2 cups brown sugar

2 cups salt

5 lbs pork belly

3 Tbsp vegetable oil

3 carrots, in ¼-inch dice

3 yellow onions, in ¼-inch dice

3 stalks celery, in ¼-inch dice

6 cloves garlic, minced

3 sprigs fresh thyme

1 tsp black peppercorns

6 cups chicken stock

This dish was inspired by the familiar bacon-wrapped scallop, which we've taken and given a twist. You can double the recipe for the molasses, or mo-lacquer, sauce and use it to grill chicken or pork. Start this dish one to two days ahead of when you plan to serve it so that you have time to cure and braise the pork belly. We serve this with roasted cauliflower purée and roasted seasonal vegetables.

BRAISED PORK BELLY Combine brown sugar and salt in a medium bowl until well mixed. Place pork belly on a baking sheet and, using your hands, pat a thick layer of the sugar-salt all over the pork belly. Cover the pork in plastic wrap and refrigerate for 12 and up to 24 hours.

Rinse pork under cold running water to remove the cure, then pat it dry with paper towels. Using a sharp knife, trim off and discard the skin. Heat vegetable oil in a large pan on high and sear pork on all sides, about 5 minutes per side. Remove from the heat and set aside.

Preheat the oven to 350°F. In a large Dutch oven, combine carrots, onions, celery, garlic, thyme, peppercorns and chicken stock and bring to a boil on medium-high heat. Add the cured pork and nestle it into the braising liquid. Cover the pot and braise for about 4 hours, until the pork is so tender it falls apart. Allow the pork to cool in this braising liquid for 2 hours.

Line a baking sheet with parchment paper. Place pork on the baking sheet (reserve the braising liquid in the pot), cover it with another piece of parchment and place a second baking sheet on top. Place a heavy weight, such as a cast-iron frying pan or large cans of vegetables on top and refrigerate for 4 to 5 hours or up to 12 hours. The pork will be pressed into a dense, compact piece.

Place a fine-mesh sieve over a clean saucepan. Pour the braising liquid through the sieve, discarding any solids. Heat the braising liquid on medium-high and reduce it to 2 cups, about 30 minutes. Set aside.

Continued overleaf…

"MO-LACQUER" GLAZE

½ cup granulated sugar

2 Tbsp water

5 Tbsp brandy

3 Tbsp molasses

3 Tbsp maple syrup

SEARED SCALLOPS

24 large scallops

Salt and black pepper

¼ cup clarified butter (page 26)

"MO-LACQUER" GLAZE Heat sugar and water in a medium saucepan on medium-high and cook until caramelized (250°F on a candy thermometer). Keeping your face away from the pan, gently add reserved reduced braising liquid, brandy, molasses and maple syrup. Reduce the heat to low and simmer for about 1 hour, or until the glaze coats the back of a spoon.

FINISH PORK BELLY Preheat the oven to 350°F. Cut pork belly into 8 pieces. Brush pork belly generously with the glaze, arrange on a baking sheet and roast for 20 minutes. Remove from the heat, brush with another coat of lacquer, cover lightly with aluminum foil to keep it moist and warm while you prepare the scallops.

SEARED SCALLOPS Pat the scallops dry with paper towels, then season with salt and black pepper. Heat clarified butter on high until hot, add scallops and fry until lightly brown and caramelized on one side, about 3 minutes. Flip scallops over and cook until lightly caramelized and golden, no more than 1 minute. Do not overcook.

TO ASSEMBLE Arrange one piece of pork belly on each plate and top with 3 seared scallops. Drizzle the plate with some of the mo-lacquer glaze and serve immediately.

Stuffed Chicken Breast with Pipérade Sauce

SERVES 6

Chicken breast stuffed, pan-fried and baked is perfect for brunch or dinner, and this pipérade sauce is also delicious as a side sauce with an omelette or grilled fish or meats. It's worth looking for passata, a drained tomato sauce with an intense flavour, at Italian or specialty food stores, where it's always sold in glass jars. Alternatively, you can make your own—see page 110. We also highly recommend roasting the red bell peppers on the barbecue so that they take on a smoky flavour, but you can roast them under the broiler or buy pre-roasted peppers in jars, if you must. A time-saving trick with fresh thyme is that you can add the whole sprig, and once the sauce has finished cooking, the stem can be removed—all the leaves will have fallen off and be cooked into the sauce.

Bon appétit.

PIPÉRADE SAUCE Preheat a barbecue to medium-high. Lightly rub bell peppers with olive oil, place them on the grill and roast, turning them frequently, until their skins are completely black, about 15 minutes. Transfer to a paper bag or a covered bowl to cool. Once the peppers are cool enough to handle, gently rub off and discard the skins and the seeds. Place the peppers in a blender and purée at high speed until smooth.

Heat olive oil and butter in a frying pan on medium. Add onions and cook until translucent and lightly golden, about 15 minutes. Deglaze the pan with red wine, scraping the bottom to remove any of the good caramelized bits, and reduce by ½, about 8 minutes. Stir in thyme, garlic, bay leaves, whole tomatoes, passata (or puréed tomatoes) and red pepper purée and bring to a simmer. Cook, using the back of a spoon to break up the tomatoes, until the sauce is reduced by roughly ½, about 15 minutes. Remove and discard the bay leaves and thyme stems, stir in fresh basil and season to taste with salt and black pepper. For a spicy pipérade, add sambal oelek or chopped chilies to taste. Set aside.

Continued overleaf…

PIPÉRADE SAUCE

4 red bell peppers

2 Tbsp olive oil, plus more for coating peppers

2 Tbsp butter

1 large onion, in ¼-inch dice

1 cup red wine

2 sprigs fresh thyme

3 to 4 cloves garlic, minced

1 to 2 bay leaves

1 can (28 oz) can whole tomatoes (we prefer San Marzano tomatoes)

2 ½ cups passata or puréed tomatoes

½ cup fresh basil leaves

Salt and black pepper

1 Tbsp sambal oelek or finely chopped red chili peppers (optional)

STUFFED CHICKEN BREAST

6 slices prosciutto

6 skinless, boneless
    chicken breasts, each 6 oz,
    refrigerated

4 to 6 oz aged cheddar,
    in 6 slices

1 cup all-purpose flour

½ tsp salt

½ tsp black pepper

3 eggs, lightly beaten

2 cups panko crumbs

¼ cup olive oil

2 Tbsp butter

STUFFED CHICKEN BREAST Preheat the oven to 375°F and turn on your exhaust fan. Line a baking sheet with parchment paper. Arrange prosciutto in a single layer and bake until crispy, 10 to 12 minutes. (The prosciutto will be very smoky.)

Reduce the oven temperature to 350°F. Set the chicken breasts on a cutting board. Using a paring knife, carefully slice into the fatter part of each breast to create an incision (not a flap) following along the middle of the breast and making sure not to cut through the sides. Stuff each incision with one slice each of prosciutto and cheese.

Combine flour, salt and black pepper on a plate. Pour the beaten eggs into a wide, shallow bowl. Set the panko crumbs on a second plate. Dredge the chicken breasts in the flour, then eggs, then panko crumbs. Make sure they are well coated. Set aside on a large plate.

In a large frying pan, heat olive oil and butter on high. Add chicken breasts and cook on both sides until golden, about 5 minutes per side. Transfer to a baking sheet and bake for 25 to 30 minutes, or until the internal temperature is 170°F. Use a meat thermometer, or insert a knife into the meat, and if the juices run clear, it is ready.

To serve, scoop a generous dollop of pipérade sauce on each plate. Cut the chicken breasts in half, on an angle, and arrange two halves on the sauce. Serve hot.

Seared Halibut on a Tomato Gratin with Pine Nut Relish

SERVES 6

Ideal for a small dinner party, the gratin can be made a day ahead and refrigerated, covered, then reheated in a 350°F oven for 10 minutes while you sear the halibut. You can also roast the pine nuts ahead of time, but assemble the relish just before serving.

TOMATO GRATIN Preheat the oven to 400°F. Line a baking sheet with parchment paper. Set an 8 x 8-inch casserole dish on a second baking sheet.

In a medium bowl, toss together tomatoes, olive oil, thyme and a pinch each of salt and black pepper. Transfer to the parchment-lined baking sheet and bake for 30 to 45 minutes, or until tomatoes have started to brown.

While tomatoes are cooking, combine garlic and cream in a small saucepan and bring to a boil on medium-high heat. Reduce the heat to low and simmer until cream is reduced by ½, about 10 minutes. Stir in parmesan. Add roasted tomatoes, season to taste and pour into the casserole dish. Cook for 10 minutes to warm through completely, then cover and set aside in a warm place.

PINE NUT RELISH Preheat the oven to 350°F. Line a baking sheet with parchment paper, arrange pine nuts on top and bake for 12 to 15 minutes, or until golden. Transfer nuts to a small bowl and mix in celery, shallots, parsley, olive oil, lemon zest, salt and white pepper.

SEARED HALIBUT Heat olive oil and butter in a frying pan on medium-high. Season halibut with salt and black pepper, then sear on one side until golden and almost cooked, 5 to 6 minutes. Turn the fish over and cook for 2 to 3 minutes more.

TO ASSEMBLE Scoop a generous spoonful of tomato gratin onto each plate, set a halibut fillet beside it and top with a dollop of relish. Serve immediately.

TOMATO GRATIN

1 ½ lbs grape tomatoes

1 Tbsp olive oil

4 sprigs fresh thyme

Salt and black pepper

1 to 2 cloves garlic, minced

1 ½ cups whipping cream

⅓ cup grated parmesan

PINE NUT RELISH

¼ cup pine nuts

¼ cup finely diced celery

¼ cup finely diced shallots

2 tsp finely chopped fresh Italian parsley

¼ cup olive oil

Zest of 1 lemon

Salt and white pepper

SEARED HALIBUT

1 Tbsp olive oil

1 Tbsp butter

6 skinless halibut fillets, each ¼ lb

Salt and black pepper

Pâté di Fegato (Tuscan Chicken Liver Pâté)

SERVES 6 TO 8

1 ½ lbs fresh chicken livers

5 Tbsp extra-virgin olive oil, plus more for brushing

½ cup finely diced red onion

¾ cup finely diced carrots

2 Tbsp finely diced celery

4 cloves garlic, 3 of them minced and 1 halved

1 tsp minced fresh parsley

2 bay leaves

½ cup Vin Santo (or any sweet dessert wine, sherry or Marsala)

Salt and black pepper

¼ cup capers, drained

1 Tbsp anchovy paste

⅔ cup unsalted butter

1 sprig fresh sage, for garnish

½ cup finely diced pancetta

1 loaf country bread or baguette, sliced

1 Granny Smith apple

My love for this simple antipasto came after an evening at Enoteca del Chianti Classico in Greve, with my wife and our good friend Stephen Smee. The proprietor, Duilio, prepared an amazing feast, including this humble pâté. As with all good Italian recipes, this one was passed down to me by Peter Bellusci, who founded Italian Gourmet Foods, the business that is now Mercato. Thanks, Peter.

Wash the chicken livers and trim off any excess fat. Set aside.

Heat 4 Tbsp of the olive oil in a saucepan on medium. Add onions, carrots, celery, minced garlic, parsley and bay leaves and cook until lightly browned, 8 to 10 minutes. Add chicken livers and sauté for 3 to 5 minutes, stirring often to ensure even cooking. Pour in Vin Santo (or other dessert wine) and allow to reduce for 5 minutes. Season with a good pinch of salt and black pepper to taste. Remove from the heat, remove and discard the bay leaves, and allow to cool for 10 minutes. Stir in capers, anchovy paste and butter, then transfer to a food processor and blend until smooth. Season to taste. Scoop the pâté into a crock, jar or serving dish and allow to cool. Garnish with a sprig of fresh sage.

While the pâté is cooling, line a plate with paper towels. Heat the remaining 1 Tbsp olive oil in a small frying pan on medium-low. Add pancetta and allow the fat to render until the pancetta is nicely browned, about 5 minutes. Transfer to the paper towel–lined plate to absorb the excess fat, then into a small dish.

Preheat the oven to 500°F. Lightly brush bread with olive oil, then grill directly on the middle rack until golden, about 4 minutes. Gently rub both sides of each piece of toast with the cut side of the halved garlic clove. Place the garlic toast in a basket.

Before serving, core the apple and slice it thinly. Place in a small dish.

To serve, arrange the dishes of pâté, pancetta, apple and bread on a large cutting board or simply in the middle of the table. Pass around individual plates and have guests assemble their own crostini by spreading the pâté generously on the bread and topping it with a little bit of apple and pancetta.

Zuppa di Pesce (Fish Soup)

SERVES 6 TO 8

PASSATA

8 cups canned whole plum
  tomatoes with juice

ZUPPA

1 ¾ lbs Manila clams

Salt

Pinch of cornmeal

¾ cup olive oil

¾ cup thinly sliced shallots

¼ cup anchovy paste (or 4 anchovy
  fillets, finely chopped)

2 Tbsp chopped fresh parsley

1 Tbsp chili flakes

¼ cup minced garlic

1 ¾ cups white wine

2 lbs halibut fillets, in 1-inch dice

6 to 8 unpeeled spot prawns
  (1 per person), rinsed well

1 lb Roma tomatoes, in 1-inch dice

6 cups water

2 tsp kosher salt

1 large wedge of lemon

1 bunch fresh basil, leaves only,
  washed and patted dry

1 baguette, in thick slices

Invented as a way to use up the unsold bits and pieces of the daily catch, Italian seafood soup is simply water, aromatics, wine and whatever variety of *frutti di mare* (seafood) you can find. In the southern regions, the addition of tomato is very common. Here is our take on *zuppa di pesce*, which has been on our menu since day one and is a favourite lunch staple with our regulars. Don't worry too much about being exact with the measurements, the types of seafood or the recipe method; as is the case for many Italian dishes, if you use fresh ingredients, the results will be delicious, whether you follow the recipe or not. Start cleaning the clams a couple of hours before you plan to serve the soup.

PASSATA Place a fine-mesh sieve over a medium bowl. Place canned tomatoes in a food processor and purée until smooth (or place the tomatoes in a large bowl and process using a handheld blender). Strain the liquid through the sieve and discard the solids. Set aside.

ZUPPA Rinse clams quickly under running water and place them in a large bowl of cold water. Throw in a handful of salt and the cornmeal, which encourages the clams to open up and spit out their sand, and refrigerate for 2 hours. Drain the clams, discarding the soaking water, and rinse thoroughly under cold running water. Set aside.

Have all the remaining ingredients ready before you begin the soup. Heat olive oil in a large, shallow saucepan on medium. Add the shallots, anchovy paste (or chopped anchovies), parsley and chili flakes and sauté, stirring constantly, until shallots begin to brown very slightly. Stir in garlic and continue cooking for another minute, until it just becomes golden. Deglaze the pot with white wine, then add clams, halibut and prawns, as well as the passata, Roma tomatoes, water and salt. Cover and allow to simmer for 5 minutes, or until all the clams have opened. (Discard any clams that do not open.)

Using the back of a large spoon, gently press down on the halibut to flake it apart. Season to taste with salt and reduce the broth or add more water, according to your preference. Ladle the soup into bowls, finish with a squeeze of fresh lemon juice, top with basil and serve with crusty bread to soak up the delicious broth.

Dungeness Crab Salad with Pork Cracklin' and Peanuts

SERVES 4

Is there anything that pork cracklin' doesn't make better? This salad is light and zippy with the lime and jalapeño dressing, and the addition of the pork cracklin' anchors the flavours with porky goodness. Pork cracklin' can be purchased at specialty meat shops—call first to make sure it's in stock—or you can use the delicious, crunchy skin from a pork roast. Serve with a glass of dry sparkling wine, such as a Crémant or a cava.

GREEN NAHM JIM DRESSING Place lemon grass, shallot, lime leaf, ginger, cilantro, garlic and jalapeños into a mortar and pound with a pestle until it forms a paste. Add the sugar, lime juice, fish sauce and salt to taste. (Will keep refrigerated in an airtight container, but use it within a couple of days or you risk the flavours becoming strong and bitter.)

DUNGENESS CRAB SALAD Place crab, cilantro, mint and shallots in a large salad bowl and mix gently until combined. Drizzle a small amount of dressing over the salad, then garnish with pork crackling and peanuts. Serve family-style.

GREEN NAHM JIM DRESSING

½ stalk lemon grass

½ shallot, peeled and roughly chopped

1 kaffir lime leaf

½-inch knob of fresh ginger, peeled and minced

3 sprigs cilantro

1 clove garlic, minced

½ jalapeño pepper, seeded and roughly chopped

2 Tbsp palm sugar (or light brown sugar)

Juice of 2 limes

5 Tbsp fish sauce

Salt

DUNGENESS CRAB SALAD

½ lb crabmeat

1 tsp chopped fresh cilantro

1 tsp chopped fresh mint

2 tsp finely diced shallots

2 tsp pork crackling

1 tsp roughly ground peanuts

Cheddar and Apple Pie

Big enough to feed a rugby team, this pie is a sweet and savoury treat. You will need a large pie dish—a 12-inch-wide, 2 ½-inch-deep cast-iron frying pan is perfect. As you cook the pie the apples almost caramelize, and the scent will have everyone gathering in the kitchen. If you're short on time, make the pie dough ahead of time and refrigerate it, wrapped in plastic, for up to 2 days. Both the pie dough and the crumble topping must be chilled for 30 minutes before baking.

PASTRY DOUGH Place flour, sugar and salt in a food processor fitted with a metal blade and pulse a few times to combine. Add butter and pulse until the mixture starts to resemble a coarse meal. With the motor running, add cheese, a bit at a time, until incorporated, then drizzle in the water and process until the dough starts to form a ball.

Lightly dust a clean work surface with flour and transfer the dough to the counter, knead it a bit, folding it over onto itself until smooth. Roll the dough into a ball, wrap it in plastic wrap and refrigerate for at least 30 minutes or for up to 2 days.

CRUMBLE TOPPING Place brown sugar, flour and salt in a food processor fitted with a metal blade and pulse a few times to mix. Add butter and pulse until the pieces are the size of small peas. Add cheese and pulse a few times until the mixture is loose and crumbly. Pour the topping into a large bowl, press it into a loose ball, wrap it in plastic wrap and refrigerate for at least 30 minutes.

Continued overleaf…

PASTRY DOUGH

4 cups all-purpose flour, plus more for dusting

1 Tbsp granulated sugar

1 tsp salt

2 cups (1 lb) unsalted butter, cold, in 1-inch cubes, plus more for greasing

3 cups grated white cheddar

1 ¼ cups cold water

CRUMBLE TOPPING

1 ¾ cups brown sugar

2 ¾ cups all-purpose flour

1 tsp kosher salt

1 cup (½ lb) unsalted butter, room temperature

1 ¾ cups aged white cheddar

APPLE FILLING

12 medium apples (we use Fujis)
½ cup (¼ lb) unsalted butter
Juice of 1 lemon
¾ cup granulated sugar
2 ½ Tbsp all-purpose flour
1 Tbsp vanilla paste

FINISH PASTRY DOUGH Preheat the oven to 375°F. Lightly grease and flour a deep 12-inch pie pan and have ready enough pie weights or dry beans to cover the bottom of the pan. Lightly dust a clean work surface with flour. Remove the dough from the fridge, unwrap it and place it on the counter. Roll out the dough until you have a circle 15 inches in diameter and ⅛ inch thick. Roll the dough around a rolling pin, then centre it over the pie pan and press it evenly into the bottom and sides. Pierce the dough in several places with a fork, fill the dish with the pie weights or beans and bake for 10 minutes, or until the crust starts to brown. Remove it from the oven, allow it to cool slightly and tip out the pie weights or beans. Set aside.

APPLE FILLING Preheat the oven to 400°F. Peel, core and slice the apples about ¼ inch thick. Melt butter in a large pot on high heat. Add apples, pour lemon juice over them and cook until softened but still crisp, about 10 minutes.

In a small bowl, combine sugar and flour until well mixed, then pour over the apples and add vanilla. Stir gently until incorporated, then pour the apple mixture into the parbaked pie shell. Cover with crumble topping, mounding it in the centre, then bake for 1 ½ to 2 hours. Serve warm.

Braised Lamb Belly with Salted Turnips and Turnip Cream

SERVES 4

Everyone's cooking with pork bellies, so why not try lamb bellies instead? Start this dish early in the day so that the lamb has time to cure and cook. Serve for dinner with a simple Côtes du Rhône.

BRAISED LAMB BELLIES In a medium bowl, combine salt, brown sugar, thyme and garlic until well mixed. Place lamb bellies in a roasting pan, spread with the herb and spice mixture, pressing it into the meat. Cover with plastic wrap and refrigerate for 5 hours to allow the meat to cure.

Preheat the oven to 300°F. Rinse lamb under cold running water to remove the salt and sugar. Set both lamb bellies on a clean work surface with the long side parallel to the edge of the counter. Starting at the edge nearest you, tightly roll up the first lamb belly to form a log. Roll up the second lamb belly in the same way. Cut 2 very long rectangles of plastic wrap. Place a lamb belly on each piece. Pull the bottom of the plastic wrap over the meat to seal it in, then roll very tightly for at least 10 rotations until you have two secure logs. Tuck the edges flat and place back up against the roll to get a tight seal. Cut two large squares of aluminum foil, one for each belly. Place a plastic-wrapped lamb belly at one edge of the foil and roll tightly into a log. Twist the ends to tighten the foil, making a firm log. Repeat with the other lamb belly. Fill the roasting pan ⅓ full with hot water, place the wrapped lamb in the pan and bake for about 3 hours, or until a meat thermometer inserted in the thickest part of the roll reads 170°F.

Fill a large stainless steel bowl with ice water. Place the wrapped lamb in it, allowing it to cool for 15 minutes. Once the lamb is cool enough to handle, unwrap and discard the foil and the plastic wrap. Using a very sharp knife, cut lamb into 1-inch-thick slices and set aside.

SALTED TURNIPS Once the lamb is cooled and sliced, set a sieve over a large bowl. Peel turnips, then use a box grater to grate them. Place grated turnip in the sieve, stir in salt and refrigerate for 1 hour, stirring every 15 minutes, until moisture has drained into the bowl.

Continued overleaf…

BRAISED LAMB BELLIES

3 Tbsp kosher salt

3 Tbsp brown sugar

2 sprigs fresh thyme, leaves only

1 clove garlic, thinly sliced

2 lamb bellies, each 8 inches long and 5 inches wide

1 Tbsp grapeseed oil

SALTED TURNIPS

4 large white turnips

¼ cup kosher salt

2 Tbsp butter

Juice of ½ lemon

2 Tbsp chopped fresh parsley

Line a plate with paper towels. Discard any moisture that has accumulated in the bowl. Rinse the colander full of turnip under cold water to remove any excess salt, then scoop the turnip onto the paper towel–covered plate to allow it to dry.

Melt butter in a large sauté pan on medium heat, add turnips and cook until tender, about 10 minutes. Remove from the heat and sprinkle with lemon juice and parsley. Cover and set aside.

TURNIP CREAM Heat olive oil in a sauté pan on medium, then add turnips and shallots and cook for 5 minutes. Add white wine and reduce the liquid by ½, about 5 minutes. Pour in water and cream and simmer for 30 to 35 minutes, or until turnips are soft and fully cooked through. Transfer the turnips and liquid to a blender and blend until smooth. Season to taste with salt.

FINISH LAMB Preheat the oven to 300°F. Heat grapeseed oil in an ovenproof sauté pan on high until it begins to smoke. Arrange lamb slices in the pan and cook for about 3 minutes per side, until golden. Transfer the pan to the oven and bake for 5 minutes.

To serve, arrange the salted turnips on a serving platter, cover with the turnip cream and rest the lamb belly beside the turnips. Serve immediately!

TURNIP CREAM

1 Tbsp olive oil
3 large white turnips, in ½-inch dice
2 shallots, thinly sliced
1 cup white wine
1 cup water
1 cup whipping cream
Salt

SERVES 4

Celeriac Soup with Pickled Red Onions

PICKLED RED ONIONS

½ cup water

½ cup granulated sugar

½ cup red wine vinegar

½ cup finely diced red onions

CELERIAC SOUP

1 Tbsp grapeseed oil

½ yellow onion, in ½-inch dice

2 stalks celery, leaves removed, in ½-inch dice

2 medium celeriac, peeled and cut in ½-inch dice

¾ cup white wine

4 cups water

¾ cup whipping cream

Salt

1 cup (½ lb) unsalted butter, in 1-inch cubes

1 apple, cored and thinly sliced (optional)

1 Tbsp ground fennel seeds, toasted (optional)

½ cup capers, drained and sautéed in 2 Tbsp grapeseed oil (optional)

Rich and creamy, this soup is delicious on its own or topped with a variety of garnishes, such as pickled red onions, brown butter, sliced apples and fennel seed, and fried capers. Choose one or choose them all—any combination makes for a great starter or lunch.

PICKLED RED ONIONS In a small saucepan, bring water, sugar and red wine vinegar to a boil on high heat. Place onions in a 4-cup pickling jar or other heatproof container with a lid, then pour the hot pickling liquid overtop. Allow the onions to cool to room temperature, then seal the container and refrigerate for up to 1 week.

CELERIAC SOUP Heat grapeseed oil in a medium pot on medium-low. Add onions, celery and celeriac and cook for 10 minutes. Pour in white wine and cook for another 2 minutes, then add water and cream. Reduce the heat to low and cook until vegetables are tender, about 45 minutes. Remove from the heat, allow to cool slightly, then pour into a blender (in batches, if necessary) and purée until silky smooth. Season to taste with salt. Set aside.

To make the brown butter, place butter in a small saucepan and simmer on medium heat until it begins to brown. Stir for 1 minute, then skim off and discard the foam. Pour melted butter into a small jar and discard the solids.

To serve, ladle hot soup into individual bowls. Top with some or all of the following: pickled red onions, brown butter, apples, fennel and fried capers. Serve immediately.

Elote (Mexican Grilled Corn)

Fresh, young, tender ears of corn with the husk and stalk still intact, folded back and tied to form a handle, are truly delicious, and this is a popular street food all over Mexico. If you want to make your own crema, start this recipe 3 to 4 days ahead, then refrigerate any leftover crema in an airtight container for up to 2 weeks; otherwise, the corn alone is quick and simple to prepare. Crema can be purchased at specialty Mexican stores such as Unimarket and should have a thick, velvety consistency. I finish the elote with Korean chili flakes for their bright, vibrant colour.

MEXICAN CREMA In a large bowl, combine cream, buttermilk, lime juice and salt. Whisk until well mixed, then cover tightly with plastic wrap. Allow to rest at room temperature or in a warm pantry for 36 hours, then refrigerate until the mixture has set, at least 12 hours. (It will have the consistency of crème fraîche.)

Line a colander with fine cheesecloth and set it over a bowl. Place the crema in the colander and allow to drain for 8 to 12 hours to remove any excess liquid. Season with more lime juice and salt to taste.

ELOTE Preheat a barbecue or grill pan to high. Wrap a strip of husk around the end of each cob, to act as a handle for the corn.

Place the corn directly on the grill and cook for about 8 minutes, rotating the cobs occasionally until cooked through. Remove from the heat and lightly season to taste with salt. Using a large spoon, spread 2 Tbsp crema evenly along each ear of corn. Sprinkle with chili powder (or chili flakes), queso fresco (or feta) and cilantro. Serve hot.

MEXICAN CREMA

4 cups + 6 Tbsp whipping cream (the higher the fat content, the better)

1 cup + 2 Tbsp buttermilk

1 Tbsp fresh lime juice

½ tsp salt

ELOTE

4 ears of fresh corn, shucked but 4 strips of husk reserved

Salt

½ cup crema

1 Tbsp chili powder or gochugaru (Korean chili flakes)

½ cup queso fresco (or feta), crumbled

¼ chopped fresh cilantro

Family-style Lamb Barbacoa

SERVES 8 TO 10

QUICK PICKLES

2 bunches red radishes,
thinly sliced

2 large red onions, thinly sliced

3 cups apple cider vinegar

4 ½ cups fresh orange juice,
strained

5 Tbsp fresh lime juice

3 tsp dried Mexican oregano

4 tsp kosher salt

3 tsp freshly ground
black pepper

SALSA ROJA

12 cloves garlic, peeled

¼ cup olive oil, plus more
for drizzling

Salt

20 long, dried guajillo peppers

4 dried chile de arbol peppers,
or more, if you like it hot

⅛ cup roughly chopped
white onions

Barbacoa is a method of cooking meat that originated in the Caribbean and may have inspired the term "barbecue." In Mexico, barbacoa typically refers to slow-cooking whole animals (lamb, goat or pig) in a pit covered with maguey leaves. With this recipe and a bit of time, you can get delicious results without digging a hole in your backyard! Use a charcoal-powered barbecue, instead. Give yourself 2 days for this recipe to allow the lamb and the pickles time to marinate, and visit La Tiendona Market, Salsita Mexican Food Market or Unimarket to pick up the various chili peppers, banana and avocado leaves and tomatillos you'll need. If you don't have time to make the salsas, you can buy them pre-made. Serve the lamb with plenty of grilled corn tortillas, cilantro and a selection of salsas and pickles for a delicious dinner party or family meal.

QUICK PICKLES Place radishes in one 3-cup mason jar and onions in another. In a medium saucepan on medium-high heat, bring apple cider vinegar, orange juice, lime juice, oregano, salt and black pepper to a boil. Pour ½ of the pickling liquid over the radishes and the other ½ over the onions. Allow to cool to room temperature, then seal the containers and refrigerate them until cold and crisp, as little as 3 hours or up to 2 days.

SALSA ROJA Preheat the oven to 350°F. Cut a square of aluminum foil large enough to hold the garlic (if you're making the salsa negra, roast those cloves now, too). Place garlic in the middle of the foil, drizzle lightly with olive oil and a pinch of salt. Bring the edges of the foil together and twist them together tightly to completely seal the package. Roast for about 20 minutes, until soft. Set aside (and reserve the 8 cloves for the salsa negra).

Continued overleaf…

MARINATED LAMB

1 lamb shoulder or leg of lamb,
    3 to 4 lbs, bone-in

Salt and black pepper

1 lb fresh banana leaves

8 to 10 dried avocado leaves

1 large carrot, roughly chopped

1 large white onion, roughly chopped

2 stalks celery, roughly chopped

1 can (330 mL) beer

2 cups water

24 to 30 corn tortillas, slightly
    warmed and toasted
    on the grill

SALSA NEGRA

2 dried chipotle peppers

1 yellow onion, peeled and
    cut in half from the top but
    with the root end intact

2 jalapeño peppers

1 fresh poblano pepper

2 medium tomatillos, husks
    removed, rinsed

2 Roma tomatoes

8 cloves garlic, roasted
    (see above)

1 Tbsp olive oil

1 packed cup roughly
    chopped fresh cilantro

2 tsp kosher salt

1 tsp ground cumin

2 tsp ground coriander

2 Tbsp fresh lime juice,
    or more to taste

Bring a small pot of water to a boil on high heat. Heat a frying pan on medium-high. Add guajillo and chile de arbol peppers in small batches and dry roast until slightly coloured and brittle, about 90 seconds. (Dry roasting brings out the full flavour and aromatics of the chili peppers.) Transfer the peppers to a small heatproof bowl, pour in enough boiling water to cover them, set a small plate on top to ensure they are fully submerged and allow to rehydrate for about 20 minutes, or until soft and pliable. Using a spoon, remove peppers, then cut out and discard the stems and seeds. Reserve the soaking water.

In a blender, combine peppers, olive oil, roasted garlic, onions and a pinch of salt and purée to a smooth, thick, velvety paste. (Add some of the reserved soaking water, as needed.) Season to taste with salt. Set aside.

MARINATED LAMB Season lamb with salt and black pepper. Scoop the salsa roja into a resealable plastic bag large enough to hold the lamb. Add lamb, seal the bag and rub the bag between your hands until lamb is liberally coated with the marinade. Refrigerate for at least 1 day, but 2 is good, too.

SALSA NEGRA Bring a small pot of water to a boil on high heat. Heat a frying pan on medium-high. Add chipotle peppers and dry roast until slightly coloured and brittle, about 90 seconds. (Dry roasting brings out the full flavour and aromatics of the chili peppers.) Transfer the peppers to a small heatproof bowl, pour in enough boiling water to cover them, set a small plate on top to ensure they are fully submerged and allow to rehydrate for about 20 minutes, or until soft and pliable. Using a spoon, remove peppers, then cut out and discard the stems and seeds. Reserve the soaking water. Set aside.

Preheat the barbecue to 425°F. Place the onion, jalapeños, poblano, tomatillos and Roma tomatoes directly onto the hot coals and cook, turning them every couple of minutes, until blackened and charred all over. Remove from the coals and allow to cool slightly. Cut out and discard the stems from the jalapeño and poblano peppers, and the root end from the onion. Roughly chop all of the blackened vegetables and transfer to a food processor. Add roasted garlic, olive oil, cilantro, salt, cumin, coriander and lime juice. Pulse until coarse and slightly chunky. Will keep refrigerated in an airtight container for up to 1 week.

FINISH LAMB Set up your grill for indirect cooking by placing the coals to one side of the grill. You will be placing the lamb on the opposite end. Heat the grill to 275°F.

Cover a baking sheet with all of the banana leaves, arranging them in a cylindrical pattern with each overlapping the next by 2 inches. Arrange ½ of the avocado leaves in the middle of the banana leaves, then remove the lamb from the marinade and set it on top. Scoop any of the extra marinade over the lamb or discard it. Arrange the remaining avocado leaves on top of the lamb. Draw the ends of the banana leaves up and over the lamb and the avocado leaves, overlapping them to "seal" the package. Secure the leaves with butcher's twine, if necessary.

Place carrots, onions and celery in a roasting pan large enough to hold a V-shaped roasting rack. Pour in the beer and water. Nestle your roasting rack in the roasting pan and place your leaf-wrapped lamb on top. Wrap the whole package tightly with foil and place on your grill. (The liquid base will help slightly steam the lamb and keep it extra moist. Wrapping it in foil will help to replicate the act of pit-roasting by keeping all the humidity and moisture inside.) Cook at 275°F for 6 hours, or until the lamb is beautifully tender and easily falls apart. Remove from the grill and allow to cool for 30 minutes.

SALSA DE AGUACATE Place tomatillos, cilantro, mint (if using), onions and serrano peppers in a food processor and pulse until coarsely chopped. Transfer to a medium bowl. Fold in avocado, lime juice, and salt to taste.

TO ASSEMBLE Unwrap the lamb, discarding the banana and avocado leaves. Arrange the lamb, hot grilled tortillas, salsa negra, salsa de aguacate and pickles on family-style platters and let the feast begin.

SALSA DE AGUACATE

8 medium tomatillos, husks removed, rinsed and quartered

¾ bunch fresh cilantro

1 small bunch fresh mint (optional)

½ large white onion, roughly chopped

4 serrano peppers, roasted, stems discarded, roughly chopped

2 avocados, mashed with the back of a fork

3 tsp fresh lime juice, or to taste

Salt

SERVES 6 TO 8

Pork Braciole (Stuffed Pork Rolls)

POMODORO SAUCE

3 Tbsp extra-virgin olive oil

½ small onion, finely diced

1 bay leaf

2 cloves garlic, minced

¼ tsp chili flakes

1 bottle (720 mL) passata

½ cup finely sliced fresh basil

Salt

BRACIOLE

1 cup day-old bread,
    roughly torn

¼ cup whole milk

2 eggs

¼ lb ground pork

¼ lb ground veal

¼ cup grated parmesan

½ cup grated smoked
    mozzarella (optional)

¼ cup chopped fresh
    Italian parsley

2 cloves garlic, minced

1 Tbsp salt

1 Tbsp black pepper

12 thin slices pounded
    pork shoulder, each ¼ lb

Salt and black pepper

12 thin slices prosciutto or
    24 thin slices pancetta

¼ cup extra-virgin olive oil

¾ cup dry white wine

Braciole is a delicious Italian roulade; the pork is stuffed with a meatball mixture, formed into a roll, then browned before being braised in tomato sauce. It also freezes really well!

POMODORO SAUCE Heat olive oil in a pot on medium, add onions and bay leaf and cook until soft and translucent, about 10 minutes. Stir in garlic and chili flakes and sauté for 2 to 3 minutes, being careful not to brown the garlic. Pour in passata, reduce the heat to very low and simmer for 30 minutes. Remove and discard the bay leaf, then stir in the basil and season to taste with salt. Set aside.

BRACIOLE To make the stuffing, place bread pieces in a small bowl and pour milk over them until moistened. In a large bowl, combine eggs, pork, veal, parmesan, smoked mozzarella (if using), parsley and garlic. Add salt and black pepper. Using your hands, squeeze excess liquid from the bread crumbs, discard the milk and add the bread mixture to the egg mixture. Mix well and set aside.

Arrange pork shoulder in a single layer on a cutting board. Season lightly with salt and black pepper. Place a slice of prosciutto (or 2 slices of pancetta) in the centre of each pork slice. Top with 2 to 3 Tbsp of bread stuffing. Starting with the edge closest to you, fold pork over the filling and roll tightly until you reach the end of the pork. Secure the roll with butcher's twine. Repeat with the remaining rolls.

Heat ½ of the olive oil in a large, heavy-bottomed Dutch oven or pot on medium. Add 6 pork rolls and brown well on all sides, about 10 minutes. Using tongs, transfer the rolls to a plate. Add the remaining oil and repeat with the last 6 pork rolls. Set aside. Reduce the heat to low, deglaze the pan with white wine and cook until reduced by ½, about 5 minutes. Add pomodoro sauce and the browned pork rolls, increase the heat to medium-low, cover and simmer for 45 minutes to 1 hour, until pork is tender and easily pierced with a fork. (You can also bake the rolls in the pomodoro sauce at 350°F for 1 to 1 ¼ hours.)

To serve, remove and discard the twine, then cut each pork roll into 4 slices. Arrange the slices on a serving platter and pour over just enough pomodoro sauce to cover them. Serve hot.

Truffled Mushroom Risotto

SERVES 4 TO 6

5 Tbsp extra-virgin olive oil, plus more for drizzling

1 lb assorted mushrooms (shiitake, portobello, chanterelle, etc.), sliced

Pinch of chili flakes

4 cloves garlic, chopped

Salt

5 Tbsp unsalted butter

1 small onion, finely diced

1 ½ cups carnaroli rice

¼ cup dry white wine

8 cups chicken stock, hot

2 Tbsp porcini powder

¾ cup grated parmesan

¼ cup chopped Italian flat-leaf parsley or chives

1 Tbsp truffle paste or 1 tsp good-quality white truffle oil

Italian comfort food at its best! You can easily make this at home and adapt it to use your favourite mushrooms. To make the porcini powder, grind dried porcini mushrooms in a coffee grinder until they have the consistency of fine dust. I prefer to use Acquerello carnaroli rice, which is found at Italian shops and specialty food stores.

Heat ¼ cup of the olive oil in a large frying pan on high (turn down the heat if the oil starts to smoke). Add mushrooms and sauté for 2 to 4 minutes, or until lightly golden and all the moisture has been released and evaporated. Reduce the heat to medium-high, stir in chili flakes and garlic and sauté for about 2 minutes, until fragrant. Lightly season with salt. Set aside.

Melt 2 Tbsp of the butter and the remaining 1 Tbsp olive oil on medium heat. Add onions and cook until softened and translucent but not browned, 8 to 10 minutes. Stir in the rice until the grains are translucent on the outside with a speck of white on the inside, about 5 minutes. Season with just a sprinkle of salt. Add white wine and stir until it evaporates, about 5 minutes.

Add 1 cup of hot stock to the rice and allow to cook, stirring continuously until all the liquid is absorbed. Continue adding stock, 1 cup at a time, stirring constantly after each addition. Repeat until the rice is still slightly hard, about 14 minutes total (you may have stock left over). Add the cooked mushrooms and porcini powder. Add the remaining stock (or water), 1 cup at a time, until the risotto is al dente, about 5 minutes. Stir in parmesan, parsley (or chives) and the remaining 3 Tbsp butter, season with salt and finish with truffle paste (or truffle oil) to taste. The rice should be creamy and moister than porridge. Spoon into individual bowls and drizzle with olive oil. Serve immediately.

Bacalao Fritters

**SERVES 4
(MAKES 10 TO 12 FRITTERS)**

½ lb salt cod
3 large Yukon Gold potatoes
¼ cup chopped parsley
2 cloves garlic, minced
Zest and juice of 1 lemon
2 Tbsp Dijon mustard
½ cup olive oil

Incredible as an hors d'oeuvre passed around before the meal or as a snack served with beer, this recipe was inspired by bacalao (salt cod) recipes from the northern coast of Spain. Our version features another layer of flavour with the addition of mustard. Start this recipe a day ahead so that you have time to soak the fish to remove the salt cure, then prepare the potatoes while the salt cod is simmering. Serve these fritters with a dipping bowl of aioli or chili paste, or both.

Place salt cod in a large bowl, cover with cold water and refrigerate overnight. Drain and discard the soaking water, and rinse the salt cod thoroughly under running water. Place fish in a medium pot of cold water and bring to a boil on medium-high heat. Reduce the heat to medium-low and simmer until fish is fork tender, about 45 minutes. Drain well, discarding the salty water. Using a fork, flake the fish and set aside.

Preheat the oven to 350°F. Place potatoes on a baking sheet and bake for about 1 hour, until easily pierced by a fork. Remove from the oven, allow to cool slightly, then scoop the flesh from the skins into a bowl. Discard the skins. Press the flesh through a potato ricer until smooth, then scoop it into a large bowl. Add flaked fish, parsley, garlic, lemon zest and juice and mustard and mix thoroughly by hand until well combined. Using a tablespoon, scoop out walnut-sized portions of the mixture and shape them into balls.

Line a plate with paper towels. Heat olive oil in a large frying pan on medium, add the balls (in batches, if necessary) and pan-fry until fritters are golden on all sides and warmed through, about 3 minutes. Using a slotted spoon, transfer the fritters to the paper towel–lined plate to drain. Arrange them on a serving platter and serve immediately.

Olive-braised Chicken

SERVES 4

Basic braised chicken showcases the simplicity and deliciousness of Spanish cooking. Serve it with roasted potatoes, crusty bread or wilted green vegetables.

Season the chicken with 1 tsp of the smoked paprika and salt, and set aside for 20 minutes at room temperature to cure.

Preheat the oven to 350°F. Heat olive oil in a large braising pan on medium. Add chicken and sear until golden on all sides, about 10 minutes. Transfer to a plate and set aside. To the same pan, add the remaining 2 tsp smoked paprika and cook for 1 minute, then stir in onions, garlic, tomatoes, bay leaf and olives (and brine) and cook until onions are soft, about 10 minutes. Deglaze the pan with white wine and chicken stock and reduce by ½, about 15 minutes. Return the chicken to the pan and add lemon zest. Bake, uncovered, for about 2 hours, or until chicken is fork tender. Allow to cool for 1 hour, then gently rewarm before serving.

4 chicken legs, about 1 lb total

3 tsp smoked paprika

2 tsp salt

¼ cup olive oil

1 onion, chopped or
    10 to 12 cippolini onions

1 clove garlic, minced

8 cherry tomatoes

1 bay leaf

1 cup mixed olives,
    with ½ cup brine

1 cup dry white wine
    (Albariño works well)

3 cups chicken stock

Zest of 1 lemon

Asian Duck Confit Drumettes with Beet-Ginger Paint

SERVES 4

CONFIT DRUMETTES

1 Tbsp Szechwan peppercorns
  + 2 tsp more, crushed, for garnish

1 ½ pods star anise,
  broken into points

3 Tbsp kosher salt

12 duck or chicken drumettes

6 cups rendered duck fat
  (if you don't have enough,
  use pastry lard to make
  up the difference)

½ bulb garlic, smashed

Zest of 1 orange

6 quarter-sized slices
  fresh ginger, smashed

1 Tbsp coriander seeds, crushed

4 green onions, in
  1-inch pieces, smashed

4 handfuls baby salad greens

Olive oil, for drizzling

The perfect appetizer! Beautiful and delicious, these drumettes pair with an off-dry Riesling or a demi-sec Chenin Blanc. We use the duck from Greens Eggs and Ham at the Crossroads Market, but you can substitute chicken drumettes and still get delicious results. You can also use duck legs, adjusting the cooking time for the bigger quotient of meat, and then serve them as a sit-down first course. Start the drumettes (or duck legs) a day ahead so that they have time to cure.

CONFIT DRUMETTES Place peppercorns, star anise and salt in a heavy frying pan and roast on medium heat, stirring until salt becomes off-white, about 5 minutes. (Adjust the heat so the peppercorns do not burn, but expect them to smoke.) Remove the spices from the heat, allow to cool slightly, then grind them to a very fine powder in a spice grinder or food processor.

Place drumettes on a plate, sprinkle with about ½ of the spice mixture and massage it thoroughly into the skin. (Store the remaining spice mixture, which makes a good dry rub, in an airtight container for use in other recipes.) Transfer the drumettes to a resealable plastic bag or a glass container tightly covered with plastic wrap and refrigerate overnight (up to 24 hours).

Preheat the oven to 350°F. Rinse the drumettes well under cold running water and pat dry with paper towels. Allow the drumettes to come to room temperature before cooking. Place them in a heavy-bottomed roasting pan.

Place duck fat in a large pot on medium-low and bring to a gentle simmer. While the fat is heating, place the drumettes in a heavy-bottomed roasting pan and add garlic, orange zest, ginger, coriander seeds and green onions. Pour the hot fat over the drumettes and simmer, uncovered, in the oven until very tender at the thickest part of the bone, about 40 minutes.

Using tongs, carefully transfer drumettes to a shallow pan. Allow the fat to cool in the roasting pan until lukewarm, about 30 minutes, then carefully strain it through a fine-mesh sieve over the duck legs. Discard the solids. (At this point, the confit can be stored for later use. Arrange the drumettes so they are completely submerged in the fat and refrigerate, uncovered, until fat congeals, then cover the container tightly and refrigerate for up to 2 weeks.)

To serve, preheat the oven to 350°F. Place drumettes in a roasting pan and cook until the fat runs off and the legs start to crisp up. Using a fork or your fingers, remove the skin from the meat and pull the meat from the bone in shreds.

BEET-GINGER PAINT Heat beet juice, red wine and honey in a small saucepan on medium and simmer for about 10 minutes, or until the liquid reduces and forms a glaze. Add a squeeze of ginger juice, discarding the solids, and season to taste with salt.

TO ASSEMBLE Drizzle each plate with 2 tsp of the beet-ginger paint or use a small, clean paintbrush to paint a large brushstroke across each plate. Top with ¼ of the greens, then carefully arrange 3 drumettes over them. Garnish with a splash of olive oil and some cracked Szechwan peppercorns.

BEET-GINGER PAINT

1 cup beet juice (juice of about 6 beets)
¼ cup red wine
2 Tbsp honey
1- to 2-inch knob of fresh ginger, grated
Salt

Verjus-poached Squid Salad with Radicchio and Chili Dressing

SERVES 4

2 ½ lbs squid tubes, cleaned

2 cups verjus

2 Tbsp honey

Sea salt and black pepper

1 head radicchio, in bite-sized pieces

1 bulb celeriac (about ¾ lb), julienned

2 navel oranges, in segments

¼ cup pitted green olives, chopped

¼ cup fresh tarragon leaves

1 clove garlic, minced

1 fresh long red chili pepper, seeded and finely chopped

2 Tbsp extra-virgin olive oil

1 Tbsp fresh lemon juice

Zest of ½ lemon

1 tsp honey

An excellent example of how quick and easy it is to make a truly unique salad. Ask your fishmonger for cleaned squid tubes. Verjus, the pressings from green grapes (sort of an unfermented wine or less acidic vinegar), is available from specialty food stores.

Using a sharp knife, cut squid into ¼-inch rings. Rinse thoroughly under cold running water. In a large saucepan, bring verjus and honey to a gentle simmer on medium heat. Add sliced squid, reduce the heat to low and cook, without boiling, for 3 minutes, or until tender. Using a slotted spoon, transfer squid to a bowl and season with salt and black pepper to taste. Discard the cooking liquid.

In a large bowl, toss radicchio, celeriac, oranges, olives and tarragon.

To make the dressing, place garlic, chili pepper, olive oil, lemon juice, lemon zest and honey in a small bowl and whisk until well combined. Season to taste with salt and black pepper.

Divide the salad mixture equally among four plates, top with poached squid and drizzle with the dressing. Serve immediately.

Roasted Carrot and Split Pea Soup with Moorish Spices, Goat Yogurt, Toasted Fennel Oil and Mint

SERVES 8 TO 10

At the River Café, we like to roast the carrots in our wood oven to add a smoky flavour, but roasting them in your electric oven is fine, too. Preserved lemons can be found at Middle Eastern groceries and specialty food stores.

Preheat the oven to 400°F. Place carrots in a large cast-iron frying pan. Add 2 Tbsp of the olive oil, season with salt and black pepper and toss until well coated. Cook for about 1 hour, stirring every 20 minutes, until well roasted and slightly caramelized. Remove from the oven and set aside.

Coat the bottom of a large pot on medium-high heat with the remaining 2 Tbsp olive oil. Add onions, shallots and garlic and cook until onions are translucent, about 10 minutes. Stir in cumin, coriander, fennel seeds, preserved lemons and chipotle peppers and sauté for 2 minutes. Add split peas, water and the roasted carrots, cover, reduce the heat to medium-low and simmer for about 1 hour, or until split peas are tender. If the soup seems too thick, add more water. (You should have about 5 qts of soup.) Stir in lemon juice and season to taste with salt and black pepper.

Just before serving, roughly purée the soup with a handheld mixer, leaving it slightly chunky. Ladle the soup into individual bowls, then garnish each serving with a spoonful of goat yogurt, a drizzle of fennel seed oil and a few strands of mint.

4 lbs carrots (we use carrots from Poplar Bluff Organics), peeled and quartered

¼ cup olive oil

Salt and black pepper

2 cups diced yellow onions

1 cup diced shallots

⅓ cup + 1 Tbsp smashed and chopped garlic

1 Tbsp ground cumin, toasted

1 ½ tsp coriander seeds, toasted and crushed

1 ½ tsp fennel seeds, toasted and ground

¼ cup + 1 Tbsp chopped preserved lemons

1 tsp minced chipotle peppers in adobo

½ cup +2 Tbsp organic yellow split peas

4 qts water

Juice of 2 lemons

¾ cup plain goat yogurt, for garnish (we prefer Fairwind Farms)

2 Tbsp toasted fennel seed oil, for garnish

10 fresh mint leaves, julienned, for garnish

Vancouver Island Savoury Clams with Bison Chorizo

SERVES 4

LOVAGE BUTTER

1 Tbsp fresh lovage leaves

½ cup (¼ lb) unsalted butter, room temperature

1 Tbsp minced shallots

1 Tbsp grainy mustard (we use brassica mustard)

CLAMS AND CHORIZO

4 lbs Savoury clams (ocean-water purged, if possible)

¼ cup cold-pressed camelina oil

1 Tbsp minced garlic

1 Tbsp minced shallots

1 ½ cups Prosecco

2 cured bison chorizo sausages, cut thinly on a bias

2 Tbsp lovage butter

¼ cup chopped fresh parsley

¼ cup chopped fresh chives

The flavour of Savoury clams marries well with bison chorizo, giving you an updated version of surf and turf. Use the freshest ingredients you can find: we use local organic products such as Vital Greens butter, Olson's High Country chorizo, Three Farmers camelina oil and herbs and vegetables from the farmers' market. Serve this dish with a large piece of grilled sourdough to soak up all the sauce.

LOVAGE BUTTER Place lovage leaves and butter in a bowl, add shallots and mustard and, using a fork, mix everything together until well combined. (This flavoured butter freezes well, rolled into a log and wrapped in plastic wrap, for up to 4 months.)

CLAMS AND CHORIZO Place clams in a colander and set it over a bowl. Rinse clams under cold running water, checking for sediment accumulating in the bowl. Dump the water from the bowl as it fills, and rinse out and discard any sediment. Keep rinsing the clams (and dumping the water in the bowl) until the water flowing into the bowl from the clams is clear. Set the cleaned clams aside.

Heat camelina oil in a deep pan on high. Add garlic and shallots and cook until the pan starts to smoke from the heat. Immediately add clams and Prosecco, then cover and steam for 1 to 2 minutes until all clams are open. (Discard any unopened clams.) Stir in chorizo, lovage butter, parsley and chives and toss until chorizo is warm and clams are coated with butter. Serve immediately.

Fried's Eggplant Sandwiches with Soft-boiled Egg and Green Tahini

SERVES 2

GREEN TAHINI

½ cup tahini

½ cup cold water

Juice of ½ lemon

½ tsp salt

½ bunch fresh parsley,
very finely chopped

5 fresh mint leaves, chopped

EGGPLANT SANDWICHES

1 eggplant

Olive oil for brushing

Salt and black pepper

2 whole eggs

2 brioche buns, sliced in half

1 red onion, thinly sliced

1 jalapeño pepper,
seeded and sliced

This is the ultimate sandwich: salty, crispy, spicy, creamy and messy. (Be sure to have lots of napkins on hand.) It was inspired by Tunisian street food, but our version is a bit more refined (and decadent) with the use of brioche, baked rather than deep-fried eggplant, and the addition of fresh mint. When choosing an eggplant, pick one that's light and has unblemished skin.

GREEN TAHINI In a small bowl, mix together tahini with water until smooth. Stir in lemon juice and salt. If the tahini is thicker than mayonnaise, thin it by adding water. Fold parsley and mint into the mixture until well blended. Will keep refrigerated in an airtight container for up to 1 week.

EGGPLANT SANDWICHES Preheat the oven to 350°F. Cut eggplant widthwise into ½-inch slices, place them on a baking sheet and generously brush both sides with olive oil. Sprinkle with salt and freshly ground black pepper. Bake for 15 to 20 minutes, then turn eggplant slices over and brush with more oil. Bake for another 15 minutes, until eggplant is soft and brown.

While the eggplant is baking, place eggs in a pot of cold water and bring to a boil on high heat. Reduce the heat to medium and cook the eggs for another 5 minutes. Remove from the heat, drain and run the eggs under cold water. Allow them to cool thoroughly in the water, then peel and set aside.

Once the eggplant is cooked, you're ready to assemble the sandwiches. Spread a generous amount of tahini on one side of each bun and layer slices of eggplant on top. Peel each egg and slice it in half. Place both halves on top of the eggplant, then top with slices of onion and jalapeño. Finally, top with another dollop of tahini, close the bun and enjoy.

Chorizo-Mango-Cilantro Pizza

**SERVES 8
(MAKES TWO 14-INCH PIZZAS)**

POOLISH PIZZA DOUGH
2 cups water, room temperature
1 tsp + ¼ tsp instant dry yeast
3 ⅚ cups all-purpose flour
1 Tbsp sea salt

This pizza is a take on the famous Hawaiian, but it's spicier, smokier and more sultry. The smokiness is embedded in the tomato sauce, the spice comes from the chorizo, the sweetness emanates from the mango and the final crispy zing is provided by fresh cilantro and lime juice. Making the pizza dough is a two-day process, which includes making "poolish"—a prefermented dough that gives the crust a deeper, more pronounced flavour. Start the poolish 12 to 16 hours before your pizza dinner, and start the tomato sauce at least an hour before using it. If you don't have time to make the dough from scratch, Italian markets, such as Mercato, also sell a pizza dough that you can use.

POOLISH PIZZA DOUGH To make the poolish, in a medium bowl, mix 1 cup of the water, ¼ tsp of the yeast and 1 ⅓ cups of the flour by hand. Loosely cover the mixture with plastic wrap and allow to stand at room temperature for 12 hours. The poolish will bubble and rise.

A couple of hours before you plan to serve the pizzas, combine the remaining 1 tsp yeast and 1 cup water in a large bowl. Add poolish, the remaining 2 ½ cups flour and salt and mix by hand until a dough forms. Do not add any more flour; the dough should be sticky. Shape it into a round, cover with a kitchen towel and allow to rise in the bowl for about 2 hours at room temperature. It should nearly double in size. (This will take longer in a colder room, less time in a warmer one.)

Divide the dough into 2 equal parts and shape it into round balls. Allow the dough to rest for 15 minutes covered with the towel. Once the dough is relaxed, stretch it into 2 round pies, each about 14 inches in diameter and ¼ inch thick. Place on a baking sheet lined with parchment paper.

SMOKY TOMATO SAUCE In a heavy pot, heat the olive oil on medium-high, then add garlic and sauté for several seconds. Stir in tomatoes and cook for 20 minutes, adding some of the tomato liquid if the tomatoes become too thick. Using a fork, crush tomatoes, then add paprika, chili flakes, salt and black pepper. Reduce the heat to medium-low and simmer the sauce for 20 to 30 minutes more, until thickened. Adjust the seasonings as needed.

TO ASSEMBLE Preheat the oven to 500°F. Brush the edges of the pizza crusts with olive oil, then generously spread tomato sauce across the centre of the dough, leaving the edges clean. Top pizzas evenly with chorizo, onions, mango and cheese. Bake until the bottom of each crust is crisp and slightly brown, about 18 minutes. Top with cilantro and a squeeze of lime juice for added flavour.

SMOKY TOMATO SAUCE

2 Tbsp olive oil

3 cloves garlic, chopped

1 can (28 oz) whole Roma tomatoes, drained but with liquid reserved

1 tsp smoked paprika

½ tsp chili flakes

Sea salt and black pepper

PIZZA TOPPINGS

Olive oil for brushing

2 fresh chorizo sausages, cooked and sliced

1 red onion, thinly sliced

1 mango, in ½-inch dice

2 cups grated full-fat mozzarella

1 bunch fresh cilantro, roughly chopped

1 lime, in wedges

SERVES 4

Ricotta Gnocchi with Brussels Sprouts and Chanterelles in a Roasted Garlic Sauce

RICOTTA GNOCCHI

4 cups all-purpose flour, plus more for dusting

2 eggs, lightly beaten

2 lbs ricotta

ROASTED GARLIC SAUCE

1 bulb garlic

1 Tbsp olive oil

¼ cup unsalted butter

2 cups button mushrooms

1 shallot, minced

2 cloves garlic, chopped

1 Tbsp soy sauce

1 cup chicken stock

The beautiful chanterelle mushroom and the muscular Brussels sprout elevate the humble gnocchi to superstar status. Note that gnocchi freezes very well. Simply arrange the cut gnocchi on a baking sheet, place it in the freezer until firm, about 45 minutes, then scoop the frozen pasta into a resealable plastic bag and keep, frozen, for up to 8 weeks. When cooking gnocchi straight from the freezer, add the pasta to the boiling water in small batches to keep the water boiling.

RICOTTA GNOCCHI Mound the flour on a large clean work surface. Make a well in the middle, add all of the eggs and the ricotta. Using a fork, slowly mix in the flour, starting from the centre of the well and working out to the edges, until you have a dough. Divide the dough in half and knead each portion gently until smooth. Do not overwork the dough. Divide each half in half again. Roll each quarter into a log about ½ inch thick and dust generously with flour. Cover the logs with a tea towel and allow to rest for 15 minutes.

Dust a clean work surface with flour. Working with one log at a time, cut into equal slices and roll them on the floured surface. Make sure all the gnocchi are well dusted and set aside.

ROASTED GARLIC SAUCE Preheat the oven to 375°F. Using a very sharp knife, cut off the top ½ inch of the garlic bulb to expose the cloves. Cut a small square of aluminum foil, set the garlic on it and drizzle with olive oil. Seal the foil tightly around the garlic and bake for about 1 hour, until completely soft and slightly brown. Set aside.

In a sauté pan on medium heat, melt butter, then add button mushrooms and shallots and cook until slightly soft, about 10 minutes. Add the chopped garlic and sauté until vegetables are soft and fragrant, about 10 minutes. Stir in soy sauce, then transfer to a food processor, purée until smooth and set aside.

Unwrap the roasted garlic and squeeze the flesh into a medium sauce-pan. Discard the foil and the garlic skin. Pour chicken stock over the garlic, bring to a boil on medium-high heat and cook until reduced by ⅔, about 15 minutes. Set aside.

BRUSSELS SPROUTS AND CHANTERELLES Fill a large bowl with ice water. Bring a large pot of water to a boil on high heat. Add Brussels sprout leaves and blanch for 4 seconds, until bright green but not cooked through. Drain immediately and transfer to the ice water. Using a slotted spoon, remove the leaves from the ice water and transfer to a plate. Pat dry with paper towels.

FINISH GNOCCHI Bring another large pot of water to a boil on high heat. Add a generous handful of salt, add gnocchi and cook until they float to the top, then continue cooking for 1 minute more. (You want the gnocchi to be relatively firm, "al dente," but no longer doughy inside.) Drain well, cover and set aside.

FINISH BRUSSELS SPROUTS AND CHANTERELLES Melt butter in a frying pan on medium-high heat. Add olive oil and chanterelles and cook until they start caramelizing, about 15 minutes. Remove from the pan and set aside.

Deglaze the pan with the reduced chicken stock and the mushroom purée. Reduce until the sauce is thick and syrupy, about 10 minutes, then add the sautéed chanterelles and heat through.

TO ASSEMBLE Place a spoonful of gnocchi on each plate, then top with a generous spoonful of the chanterelles and sauce and a spoonful of crème fraîche. Sprinkle Brussels sprouts overtop and finish with parmesan and a squeeze of lemon juice. Serve immediately.

BRUSSELS SPROUTS AND CHANTERELLES

4 cups Brussels sprouts, separated into individual leaves or slivered with a mandoline

¼ cup butter

2 Tbsp olive oil

7 cups chanterelle mushrooms, sliced

⅓ cup crème fraîche

1 ½ cups grated parmesan

½ lemon, in 4 wedges

SERVES 8 TO 10

Smoked Pork Rib Chops with Caramelized Applesauce

SMOKED PORK RIB CHOPS

8 cups water

1 ½ cups salt

5 pods star anise

2 ½ Tbsp fennel seeds

2 ½ Tbsp coriander seeds

1 Tbsp chili flakes

⅔ cup fancy molasses

4 lbs ice (optional)

1 pork rack, 12 lbs, bone in,
    cleaned and skin removed
    but with a good layer of
    fat left on

1 lb applewood chips

SWEET APPLESAUCE

1 cup (½ lb) butter

8 Granny Smith apples,
    peeled, cored and halved

½ cup brandy

1 cup chicken stock

1 cup veal demi-glace

The best things in life are worth waiting for, and smoked pork rib chops are no exception. Give yourself at least 2 days to make this dish, as the pork has to brine for 24 hours. If you don't have a smoker, fake it and put hardwood chips (available at hardware and barbecue stores), wrapped in aluminum foil, underneath the cooking grate of your grill, then roast and smoke the meat. Serve with grilled polenta and an arugula salad, then open a bottle of Chianti and you have a great meal!

SMOKED PORK RIBS In a large stockpot, bring water, salt, star anise, fennel seeds, coriander seeds, chili flakes and molasses to a boil on high heat. Set aside to cool completely, or if you are in a hurry, pour in the ice to cool it completely. Place pork ribs in a large pan, add brine until well covered, refrigerate and allow to cure for 24 hours.

Preheat the smoker to 200 to 225°F. Soak the wood chips in water for 15 minutes, then drain and place them in the smoker. (Each smoker is different, so follow the instructions on yours.) Pour off and discard the brine. Rinse the pork under cold running water, then thoroughly pat dry with paper towels. Place the pork rack in the smoker, close it and smoke for 6 hours. The intent is to impart a smoky flavour without cooking the pork rack. Remove the meat from the smoker, wrap it in aluminum foil and set it aside to rest for 30 minutes.

SWEET APPLESAUCE Melt butter in a large saucepan on medium-high heat. When it begins to sizzle, add apples, reduce the heat to medium and cook, caramelizing the apples, for about 45 minutes. Transfer to a bowl and set aside. Deglaze the pan with brandy and chicken stock and veal demi-glace, making sure to scrape the bottom to get all the caramelized bits. Transfer to a food processor and purée until smooth.

FINISH PORK RIB CHOPS Preheat a barbecue to 425°F. Slice the rack into 2-bone servings. Grill for 15 minutes, or until the meat reaches an internal temperature of 135°F. (Use a meat thermometer inserted in the meaty part of the chop.) Brush the ribs with applesauce just before they are finished cooking. Place each portion of ribs on a plate, with spoonfuls of applesauce on the side. Serve immediately.

Tiramisù

SERVES 12

The Italians know a thing or two about dessert, and the classic tiramisù is a treat that everyone looks forward to. Perfect for a large group, this recipe serves 12 people and can be made a day ahead. Serve with strong coffee or a small glass of liqueur.

3 egg whites
½ cup granulated sugar
1 ¼ cups whipping cream
1 cup mascarpone
6 egg yolks
2 Tbsp vanilla paste
3 sheets gelatin
24 ladyfinger biscuits, halved
½ cup brewed espresso
¼ cup Amaretto, Kahlua or Sambuca
1 Tbsp good-quality chocolate powder, for dusting

In the bowl of a stand mixer fitted with a whisk attachment, whip egg whites and ¼ cup of the sugar until it forms soft peaks, about 5 minutes. Scrape the meringue into a small bowl and refrigerate until chilled. Rinse off the mixing bowl and the beaters.

Place 1 cup of the cream in the mixing bowl and whip into soft peaks, about 5 minutes. Scrape into a small bowl and refrigerate until chilled. Rinse out the mixing bowl once again and fit the mixer with the paddle attachment.

Place the mascarpone and the remaining ¼ cup sugar in the mixing bowl and beat until creamy and soft, scraping down the side to ensure there are no lumps, about 8 minutes. With the motor running, slowly add egg yolks, one at a time. Once all the yolks are fully incorporated, scrape down the bowl with a spatula, add vanilla paste and mix until thoroughly combined. Refrigerate until chilled and ready to assemble.

Place the gelatin in a small bowl and add just enough water to cover. Allow to sit for 10 minutes or until slightly softened.

Heat the remaining ¼ cup cream in a medium saucepan over high heat until very hot but not boiling, then add the gelatin and stir until completely dissolved. Slowly pour the hot cream into the mascarpone mixture and combine thoroughly. Transfer the mixture to a large bowl, fold in the whipped egg whites, then the whipped cream.

Line the bottom of a 12-inch glass casserole dish with the ladyfingers. In a small bowl, combine the espresso and liqueur and brush the ladyfingers with just enough of this mixture to moisten them. Spread the cream topping over the ladyfingers, dust with chocolate and refrigerate for about 4 hours or as long as overnight. Cut into slices and serve chilled.

Beef Tenderloin and Soft Polenta

SERVES 4

3 Tbsp olive oil

1 ½ to 2 lbs trimmed
beef tenderloin

2 ½ cups chicken stock

2 ½ cups whole milk

1 cup cornmeal

¼ cup butter

¼ cup mascarpone

Salt and black pepper

Polenta is an easy, satisfying comfort food, made even better by pairing it with a beef tenderloin. Serve at dinner with a crisp salad or seasonal vegetables.

Preheat the oven to 450°F. Heat olive oil in a large frying pan on medium-high. Add beef and sear until browned, about 5 minutes per side. Transfer beef to a baking sheet and cook in the oven for 5 minutes for rare (or 8 minutes for medium rare). Remove beef from the oven and allow to rest for 5 minutes.

While the beef is resting, make the polenta. In a large pot, combine chicken stock and milk and heat on medium-high. Gradually whisk in cornmeal and cook, stirring, until the grains are soft and completely incorporated, about 15 minutes. Fold in the butter and mascarpone and season to taste with salt and black pepper.

To serve, mound the polenta in the middle of each plate (or in the centre of a family-style platter). Cut the beef into 4 portions, rest them against the polenta, spoon over some of the pan juices and serve immediately.

Kale Caesar Salad

SERVES 4

This kale concoction started as a garnish at UNA. People loved it so much that we turned it into a full salad. It's been the number one seller at UNA ever since.

CAESAR DRESSING Using a fork, crush garlic and anchovies against the inside of a large bowl. Add mustard, lemon juice and zest and olive oil and whisk until well emulsified. Pour the dressing into a glass jar and set aside.

KALE SALAD Line a plate with paper towels. Heat olive oil in a medium frying pan on high. Add prosciutto and pan-fry until crispy, about 5 minutes. Transfer to the paper towel–lined plate and set aside. Reduce the heat to low.

Add panko crumbs to the pan, adding a little oil if required, and toast until golden, about 2 minutes. Scrape the panko into a small bowl, season to taste with salt and set aside.

Place kale in a large bowl, pour in the dressing and toss well. Season with salt and black pepper. Transfer to a serving bowl and top with Pecorino Romano, toasted panko and crispy prosciutto. Serve with the boiled eggs, if desired.

CAESAR DRESSING

1 clove garlic
4 anchovy fillets
1 Tbsp Dijon mustard
Zest and juice of 1 lemon
½ cup olive oil

KALE SALAD

2 Tbsp olive oil, plus more, if needed
4 thin slices prosciutto, julienned
½ cup panko crumbs
Maldon salt and black pepper
2 bunches kale, leaves only, julienned
1 cup grated Pecorino Romano
2 soft-boiled eggs, peeled and halved (optional)

UNA's Famous Meatballs

SERVES 4 TO 6

¼ cup whole milk

¼ cup panko crumbs

½ lb ground veal

½ lb ground pork

¼ cup ground prosciutto

2 Tbsp extra-virgin olive oil

1 tsp chili flakes

1 Tbsp minced garlic

¼ cup chopped fresh parsley

Kosher salt

¼ cup grated parmesan +
    ¼ cup more for garnish

4 cups passata

1 chunk parmesan rind,
    about 6 inches, broken
    into large pieces

These meatballs have been on the UNA menu from day one. I borrowed a technique from famous Calgary cook Cath Caracciolo and then developed our own ratio of veal, pork and prosciutto. The key technique is using parmesan rinds in the braise to add a tremendous depth of flavour. Find passata, a drained tomato sauce sold in glass jars at Italian or specialty food stores, or make your own (see page 110). Serve the meatballs hot with freshly grated parmesan, olive oil and toasted bread.

MEATBALLS Preheat the oven to 350°F. Combine milk and panko crumbs in a medium bowl and allow to soak for 20 minutes. In a large bowl, mix veal, pork, prosciutto, olive oil, chili flakes, garlic, parsley, salt and parmesan until well combined, then add the panko mixture and stir thoroughly to incorporate.

Preheat the oven to 350°F. Using your hands, shape the meat mixture into golf-sized balls and place them in a roasting pan, leaving a little space around each one. Pour in passata and add the cheese rind. Add just enough water to cover the meatballs and sauce. Bake for about 2 hours, remove from the heat and remove and discard the cheese rind. Arrange meatballs on a large platter or on individual plates and garnish with grated parmesan. Serve immediately.

Open-faced Spicy Tuna Melts

SERVES 4

The spicy tuna melt is the answer to those times when you're craving the queen of tuna sandwiches. It is warm, spicy and rich, is easy to make and probably won't require a shopping trip. Try the tuna melt for lunch with a bowl of soup and a bottle of stout.

Preheat the broiler on the oven. In a bowl, mix tuna, mayonnaise, red onions and celery until well combined. Stir in hot sauce and season to taste with salt and black pepper. Spread the tuna mixture evenly over the two halves of the baguette and sprinkle with the grated cheeses. Place the sandwiches on a baking sheet and broil, using the lowest rack so that you can warm the tuna without burning the cheese, until cheese has browned, about 5 minutes. Remove from the oven, top with green onions and cut each of the baguette halves in two. Serve hot, open faced, on individual plates.

1 can (13 oz) flaked
    white tuna, drained
1 cup mayonnaise
1 Tbsp chopped red onions
1 Tbsp chopped celery
1 tsp hot chili paste
    (Sriracha is good)
Salt and black pepper
1 fresh baguette, cut lengthwise
¼ cup grated Gruyère
¼ cup grated cheddar
¼ cup chopped green onions

Butternut Squash Velouté

SERVES 4

½ cup + 2 Tbsp butter

2 Tbsp olive oil

1 onion, in ¼-inch dice

1 carrot, cut in ¼-inch rounds

1 stalk celery, in ¼-inch pieces

Salt

2 lbs butternut squash, peeled and cut in ¼-inch dice

2 ½ cups vegetable broth

¼ cup mascarpone

Brown sugar to taste

Crème fraîche, for garnish

Micro sprouts for garnish

Pinch of Maldon salt, for garnish

It is said that a good soup is the sign of a good cook, and velouté, which roughly translates to "velvet," will garner you many compliments. Serve this luscious soup in tiny cups as an amuse-bouche at a dinner party or in larger bowls with slices of your favourite crusty baguette as a meal.

Melt 2 Tbsp of the butter in a large sauté pan on medium-high heat, then add olive oil. Stir in onions, carrots and celery and a pinch of salt and sauté until onions are translucent and carrots and celery are soft, about 10 minutes. Add squash and sauté until soft and easily pierced with a fork, about another 10 minutes. Add enough vegetable broth to completely cover the vegetables, then allow the soup to come to a boil. Reduce the heat to medium-low and simmer for about 15 minutes, until squash is completely soft and thoroughly cooked.

Using a handheld blender or a food processor, purée soup on high speed until smooth. With the motor running, slowly add the remaining ½ cup butter and the mascarpone until smooth and well incorporated.

Transfer the soup to a clean pot and simmer on medium-high heat to warm it through. Season with a little brown sugar and salt to taste. Serve hot in individual bowls. Garnish with crème fraîche, micro sprouts and Maldon salt.

Dungeness Crab and Grapefruit Salad with Coconut Lime Dressing

SERVES 4

Cool, crunchy and slightly spicy, this salad is ideal with Crispy Calamari with Ancho Chili Mayo (page 37) and a glass of chilled, off-dry Pinot Gris. Vary the presentation of this salad by layering the ingredients and drizzling the dressing overtop as we do in the restaurant. And use any leftover coconut lime dressing with grilled salmon.

COCONUT LIME DRESSING Heat olive oil in a large sauté pan on medium-high. Add lemon grass, ginger, shallot and lime leaves until fragrant, about 10 minutes. Turn off the heat, add coconut milk and allow to steep for 15 minutes. Stir in lime juice and chili paste until smooth. Slowly add canola oil in a steady stream, whisking constantly until dressing is emulsified. (Adding too much oil too quickly can cause the dressing to separate.) Stir in salt and yogurt until well combined. Adjust seasonings, adding more salt as needed. Set aside and refrigerate for 1 to 2 hours. Just before serving, pour the dressing through a fine-mesh sieve into a clean jar. Discard the solids. Will keep refrigerated in an airtight container for up to 1 week.

CRAB SALAD In a large bowl, combine crab, apples, grapefruit, lettuces and radishes. Pour the dressing over the salad and toss well. Divide the salad evenly among 4 plates, and serve immediately.

COCONUT LIME DRESSING

2 Tbsp olive oil

1 stalk lemon grass, finely diced

2 tsp finely diced fresh ginger

½ shallot, thinly sliced

2 lime leaves

1 cup coconut milk

¾ cup fresh lime juice

½ Tbsp hot chili paste (Sriracha or sambal oelek)

1 cup canola oil

1 tsp salt

1 Tbsp plain full-fat yogurt

CRAB SALAD

1 lb fresh Dungeness crabmeat

½ Granny Smith apple, cored and thinly sliced

1 grapefruit, in segments

1 head butter lettuce, leaves separated in bite-sized pieces, washed and patted dry

1 head red leaf lettuce, leaves separated in bite-sized pieces, washed and patted dry

2 radishes, thinly sliced

Baked French Onion Soup with Braised Oxtail

SERVES 6 AS A STARTER OR 4 AS A MAIN COURSE

1 Tbsp vegetable oil

1 beef oxtail

Salt and white pepper

8 cups unsalted beef or chicken stock

3 Tbsp unsalted butter

2 cloves garlic, thinly sliced

2 lbs yellow onions, thinly sliced

2 tsp all-purpose flour

1 cup dry white wine

Herb sachet (2 sprigs fresh Italian parsley, 2 sprigs fresh thyme, 8 black peppercorns, 1 bay leaf tied in a cheesecloth bag)

2 Tbsp sherry

4 to 6 thick slices of brioche (1 per serving)

4 to 6 medium-thick slices Gruyère

French onion soup has been described as culinary alchemy: creating gold out of the humble onion and oxtail. Serve this classic soup for lunch or dinner.

Preheat the oven to 350°F. Heat vegetable oil in a large sauté pan on medium. Season oxtail with salt and white pepper, add it to the pan and sear, cooking all sides, until golden and caramelized, 10 to 15 minutes. Transfer oxtail to a large roasting pan, add beef (or chicken) stock and braise for 2 to 3 hours, until soft and tender. Transfer the oxtail to a plate, cover and refrigerate while you prepare the onion soup. Set a fine-mesh sieve over a clean bowl and pour the braising liquid through it. Discard the solids, pour the liquid into an airtight container and reserve for use in place of stock in another recipe. Will keep refrigerated in an airtight container for up to 1 week.

Melt butter in a large pot on medium. Add garlic and onions, season with salt and white pepper and cook, stirring continually for 30 to 40 minutes, until onions are a rich brown but not burned. Dust the onions with flour and continue to stir for 5 minutes more. Pour in white wine, then add the herb sachet and cook until the white wine is almost completely evaporated, about 10 minutes.

Shred the oxtail meat and add it to the soup. Reduce the heat to medium-low and allow the soup to simmer, regularly skimming fat and other impurities off the top, for 30 to 40 minutes. Remove and discard the sachet, add sherry and adjust the seasonings. Simmer the soup for 10 or 20 minutes more.

Preheat the oven to 350°F. Arrange brioche slices on a baking sheet and toast in the oven until golden, 8 to 10 minutes. Remove from the oven and season with salt and white pepper. Increase the oven temperature to 450°F. Ladle soup into individual ovenproof bowls. Top each brioche with a slice of cheese, then place one brioche crouton in each bowl. Set the bowls on a baking sheet and place in the oven, watching them closely until cheese melts and becomes golden. Serve immediately.

THE CHEFS

The Chefs

Añejo

Añejo on 4th Street SW is the sister restaurant of The Living Room on 17th Avenue SW. Of the two, Añejo is the one you'd want to party with, as it brings fun, tequila and regional Mexican food to Calgary's Mission neighbourhood. The partners—Patrick Hill, Michael Miller, Cliff Harvey, Jeff Hines and Kevin Hill—travelled to Mexico to research foods, then returned home to Calgary, put a skull in the window of the restaurant and were surprised by how many résumés they received from the city's large Latino and Mexican community. In keeping with its philosophy of interactive food, Añejo offers many shared plates and fantastic, table-side guacamole.

01 KEVIN A. HILL

Born and raised in Calgary, Executive Chef Kevin Hill has always believed in the power of local, regional produce and meat. Fifteen years ago he started a business to introduce organic, local, wholesome foods to residents of Black Diamond, but it was ahead of its time. He moved to Calgary and worked at The 400 Club before starting at The Living Room eleven years ago. Thanks to Kevin's rich knowledge of foods and a kitchen staffed with many Mexican cooks, the ingredients and techniques at Añejo are true to their authentic Mexican roots.

Anju Restaurant and Lounge

Anju, which means "tapas, or a dish eaten with alcohol," is located on 17th Avenue SW. Specializing in Korean food, the award-winning restaurant features fresh, healthy, flavourful and traditional dishes with a modern twist inspired by Korean and Canadian cultures. It offers many shared plates, and *soju,* a Korean rice alcohol similar to vodka, is the recommended beverage of choice.

02 ROY OH

Originally from Edmonton, Chef Roy Oh moved to Calgary a decade ago armed with a degree in visual communications. He eventually discovered that he loved cooking more than drawing. A self-taught chef, he has improved his techniques by working with some of the best chefs in Calgary, including Model Milk's Justin Leboe and Teatro's John Michael MacNeil. He wants to change the way you think about food, to open your mind to new flavours and possibilities and to create community and embrace his roots by serving shared plates, encouraging people to come together by eating together.

Avec Bistro

Owned by Jackie Cooke, Kirk Shaw and Gail Norton, Avec Bistro is part of Calgary's thriving French food scene. Its zinc bar, bistro-inspired menu and extensive wine list create a fresh, salon-like gathering place in Calgary's Design District. Floor-to-ceiling windows look out onto the patio and provide plenty of light and window seating. The recent addition of an antique absinthe fountain will provide fuel for conversation well into the night.

03 DILAN DRAPER

Dilan Draper grew up in Calgary and entered SAIT's culinary program. He quickly got the urge to travel after recruiters from Le Cordon Bleu came to town, and immediately transferred to San Francisco and then Paris to complete his training. He returned to Calgary and took a position at Da Capo and then Bistro La Persaud in Edmonton, followed by the Michelin-starred Waterloo & City in Culver City, California. Other stops include Ortolan and Guy Savoy (Paris) and Fleur De Sel in Nova Scotia. Dilan returned to Calgary in 2013 to set down roots and take on the role of running a team and kitchen.

The Beltliner

The newly opened diner is a true neighbourhood joint. Bright, cheery and comfortable, it's a modern take on the diner concept serving upscale comfort food that is local, organic and house-made. The Beltliner is casual and approachable with the chops to throw down some *serious* food while trying to make booze for breakfast more of a thing. It's Calgary's go-to place for breakfast-lunch-dinner and late night.

04 SHAWN GREENWOOD

A native of B.C., Executive Chef Shawn Greenwood has been living in Calgary for the last fifteen years and banging around in kitchens since he lied about his age to get his first dishwashing job. He has a great love of eating animals and animal products and has never been seen purposely eating a vegetable. His food often takes on classic items or pop culture references; for example, Kool-Aid crème brûlée is a favourite. The owner and operator of one of Calgary's first food trucks (The Perogy Boyz), he made *Western Living* magazine's list of the top 40 foodies under 40 in 2011.

Blink Restaurant & Bar

Blink Restaurant & Bar is located on the Stephen Avenue mall in downtown Calgary. The restaurant's carefully considered menus—which emphasize local, sustainable produce, organic hormone-free meats and Ocean Wise seafood—and extensive wine list reflect owner and director Leslie Echino's love of travel and twenty-two years of experience in the restaurant and fine dining business, as does its industrial warehouse loft feel, which combines brick walls, high ceiling, hardwood floors as well as comfortable tables and flattering lighting to create intimacy in the open space.

05 CHRISTOPHER DEWLING

Christopher Dewling has been the executive chef since 2011 and was the sous-chef for two years before that. Born in St. John's, Newfoundland, he did a stage with Chef Philip Howard in London's The Square, learning about European cooking and techniques, and moved to Calgary in 1999. A proponent of the Slow Food Movement, Christopher supports small, local businesses focussing on regional cuisine.

Bonterra Trattoria

Calgary's lively Bonterra Trattoria channels the spirit of Italy with its Tuscan-themed terrace; its wine room, which is available for private events; and classic and contemporary cuisine that combines Italian meats and cheeses with local ingredients. It is perfect for an informal meal, romantic evening or business lunch.

06 GLEN MANZER

Growing up in Winnipeg, Glen Manzer spent many an evening cooking with his grandmother. Now chef and partner with Creative Restaurants, working at Cibo and Bonterra, he has been sourcing local, regional meats and produce and building relationships with farmers since way before it was cool. He also now enjoys coaching and teaching the next generation of chefs and spending time with his daughter. Glen's creative Italian menus emphasize simple, fresh ingredients.

Brûlée Patisserie

Brûlée is a Calgary favourite. Located downstairs on 11th Ave SW in the heart of the Design District, the patisserie is a must-stop shop for lovers of cakes, cookies, squares and sticky buns. On Saturdays the shelves are lined with savoury items like quiches, croissants, focaccia and savoury muffins, but everything is snapped up by noon, so get there early! During the Christmas season the bakers work all night and day, stopping only for the occasional, fortifying glass of wine.

07 JENNIFER NORFOLK

Jennifer Norfolk started her baking career by packing boxes at Dr. Cheese and The Cake Lady in Toronto and then was promoted to baking. After a detour into archival work with the CBC, she remembered the lure of baking and took a job at Brûlée in 1997. Now the owner of the popular bakery, she makes classic homemade desserts that appeal to the senses and connect with the emotions. They are designed to look, taste and smell even better than the ones you remember!

Candela Lounge

Candela, the sister restaurant to Alloy Fine Dining Restaurant, has a globally influenced, shared-plates menu that's a favourite of tapas-loving Calgarians. Dishes inspired by Latin, Mediterranean and Asian flavours complement a fun, fresh cocktail and wine list. The beautiful main space, designed by owner Uri Heilik, is built around a large, centrally located rectangular bar that anchors the room under a huge skylight. Large windows look onto 4th Street SW, and you can't help but notice the beautiful Moroccan lights illuminating the private dining room.

08 ROGELIO HERRERA

Co-owner and chef Rogelio Herrera started out washing dishes, became a line cook, realized he had great instincts and skills and fell in love with cooking. Mostly self-taught, Rogelio took a few cooking courses but has learned the most from being in kitchens, learning through trial and error what works and what doesn't. Rogelio's cuisine is influenced by his Latin roots and his love of Asian ingredients and Mediterranean culture.

05

06

07

08

Cassis Bistro

Born near Aix-en-Provence in the south of France, owner and operator Gilles Brassart grew up in the kitchen surrounded by simple, fresh flavours that fuelled his passion for food. In 2008, following two successful restaurant projects in San Francisco, Gilles arrived in Calgary and three years later founded Cassis Bistro. The restaurant features authentic cuisine from the south of France. Located in Casel Marché, Cassis Bistro uses fresh, seasonal and most often organic meat and produce from local farmers and ranchers.

09 DOMINIQUE MOUSSU

Executive Chef and partner Dominique Moussu hails from Brittany, France, and apprenticed at a Michelin-star restaurant after graduating from the Brevet d'Etudes Professionelles. He has cooked in top luxury hotels, including The Savoy in London, and was executive chef and managing partner at Teatro in Calgary before opening L'Épicerie in 2008. Bringing Dominique's award-winning vision to life on the plate every day is Head Chef Jean-Philippe Charpentier, who grew up in the heart of Southern France, knows the local ingredients and techniques and is uniquely suited to bring out the best in Cassis's cuisine.

Shown with J-P Charpentier in photo

Catch & The Oyster Bar

Open since 2002, Catch & The Oyster Bar was Calgary's first seafood restaurant to capture the essence of both the east and west coasts. Located downtown in the Imperial Bank Building, the grand space is friendly and inviting. Voted the Best Seafood Restaurant by *Avenue Magazine* in 2011, Catch uses fresh 100 per cent sustainable, Ocean Wise seafood. The restaurant also maintains a rooftop garden and beehives.

10 KYLE GROVES

Kyle Groves was born in Calgary and has travelled and worked in award-winning and Michelin-starred restaurants and hotels throughout Scotland and England. While living in Vancouver, he did dinner and events at the Vancouver Aquarium. Voted one of Calgary's top 40 under 40 in 2013, Kyle emphasizes education, supports the "learning kitchen" concept and attended the first-ever National Sustainable Seafood Day with David Suzuki in March 2014.

CHARCUT Roast House

CHARCUT Roast House presents "back-to-basics" food expertly prepared, fresh and from scratch. This is the place for house-made meats, homemade preserves and the freshest produce, much of it grown in the kitchen garden. The extensive wine and drinks list is complemented by a menu that changes daily. Lauded across the country, the award-winning restaurant raises funds and awareness for a range of charities. The owners also operate Alley Burger Food Truck, and their second venture, charbar, opens in 2015.

11 JOHN JACKSON AND CONNIE DESOUSA

Co-owners and co-executive chefs John Jackson and Connie DeSousa met and worked together in Calgary, then opened San Francisco's prestigious Mobil Five-Star St. Regis Hotel, before returning to Calgary to open their first venture in 2010. John staged at London's River Café and Paris's Le Jardin des Cygnes and studied artisanal sausage-making in Italy's Marche; Connie at New York's Jean-Georges and San Francisco's Quince. She honed her butchery skills in Berkeley at Chez Panisse. She was a finalist on Food Network Canada's *Top Chef Canada* and is recognized as one of Canada's finest female chefs.

Chef's Table

The Kensington Riverside Inn, sister restaurant to Yellow Door, is Calgary's only member of the Relais and Châteaux network of luxury boutique hotels dedicated to the highest standards of service. It is home to Chef's Table, one of Calgary's finest restaurants. Executive Chef Duncan Ly and sous-chefs Daniel Labutes and Michel Nop lead the AAA Four-Diamond award-winning restaurant specializing in French modern cuisine. The wine program, led by Maître d'hôtel Guillaume Frélot, concentrates on smaller, eclectic producers that pair brilliantly with the gourmet cuisine.

12 DANIEL LABUTES AND MICHEL NOP

Daniel Labutes began cooking professionally in 2007, graduated from NAIT's Culinary Arts program in 2009 and moved to Calgary in 2011. Daniel joined Chef's Table in August 2012, prior to which he was the sous-chef at Cassis Bistro. Michel Nop was born and raised in Paris, France, where he was classically trained at some of Europe's top restaurants. In Calgary, he worked at Cassis Bistro, Teatro and Catch before joining the team at Chef's Table. Daniel and Michel uphold the highest standards while making others happy through their cooking.

Shown with Duncan Ly in photo

The Cookbook Co. Cooks

The Cookbook Co. Cooks has been a culinary hub for Calgarians since 1984. The 11th Avenue location features retail space for specialty foods, kitchenware and cookbooks plus a cooking school that hosts hundreds of cooking classes, wine classes, specialty dinners and workshops each year, given by the best chefs, food professionals and authors in Calgary and guest chefs from across Canada. The cooking classes are casual, entertaining and informative, and the store has become a gathering place for people who love to cook and eat good food.

13 MATTHEW ALTIZER

From the time he was three years old and attempted to roast his baby blanket, Matthew Altizer knew he would be a chef. He started working at The Cookbook Co. when he was thirteen and earned Global knives for good grades in school. He later attended the Pacific Institute of Culinary Arts, where he graduated with the school's highest practical marks. Travelling in Mediterranean countries, especially Morocco, where similar ingredients are used in different ways to create deep, savoury flavours has influenced his cooking. Matthew has cooked for Anthony Bourdain, Margaret Atwood and Eric Ripert of New York's Le Bernardin.

The Coup

Located on trendy 17th Street sw, The Coup is dedicated to providing creative vegetarian fare in a fun, vibrant atmosphere and promoting local, whole, healthy organic food. Simple, modern décor complements the ethical food philosophy, and the restaurant is 100 per cent wind powered and plants thirty-six trees a month to offset its waste. The cooks bring their own unique style, experience and knowledge to the kitchen, creating fresh, bold, flavourful food, perfect accompaniments to a freshly juiced cocktail or a glass of organic wine.

14 DALIA KOHEN

While working at a local diner, and after serving the breakfasting hordes plates of pork product, Dalia Kohen decided there was a place for a great vegetarian restaurant in Calgary. She opened The Coup in 2004, using her experiences from travelling and working in bars, diners, restaurants and cafés. Mostly self-taught in the kitchen, her cuisine is influenced by big, bold fresh flavours, drawn from cultures around the world and made from sustainable, locally sourced products that are organic, biodynamic and fair trade with minimal packaging. Not unsurprisingly, Calgarians have embraced The Coup's meals without meat.

Craft Beer Market

Craft Beer Market puts the "think global, support local" philosophy front and centre by pairing fresh local food with locally produced beer. By purchasing sustainably grown produce and humanely raised animals, the restaurant supports the local economy and creatively incorporates seasonal produce into the menu, all the while offering Calgarians Canada's largest selection of draft beer in three boisterous, comfortably buzzing locations. How can we resist?

15 PAUL McGREEVY

Corporate chef Paul McGreevy is a graduate of SAIT's Culinary Arts program and spent three years travelling and gaining experience and new ideas from kitchens in Northern Ireland, France and his favourite country, Italy. Returning to Calgary, he headed the kitchen at Wildwood Restaurant and the Vintage Group before becoming the executive chef at Craft. His goal is to continue locating the best local ingredients and offering innovative food and drink in a fun, relaxed setting.

Cucina

Cucina means "kitchen" in Italian. Open for breakfast, lunch and dinner, Cucina changes its menu daily but always includes an offering from the chicken rotisserie. Whether diners are sipping an espresso or enjoying a glass of wine at the bar, ordering "grab and go" specialty coffees and fresh baked goods at the market café, gathering around the harvest table with a large group of friends or dining in the Italian Bistro, Cucina's warm, rustic atmosphere brings heart and soul to downtown Calgary.

16 ROMUALD COLADON

Executive Chef Romuald Coladon was raised and trained in France and came to Calgary by way of Montreal, where he worked at the renowned Les Caprices de Nicolas and Decca 77. Formerly the chef at Teatro, he is known for elegant but simple Italian cuisine made with a light-handed style and technique. Sourcing the highest-quality local ingredients from organic, sustainable producers where possible, he brings vibrant, creative energy to Cucina's open, airy kitchen.

17

18

19

20

Cuisine et Château

Cuisine et Château's state-of-the-art Interactive Culinary Centre is located in Calgary's Kensington district and provides hands-on cooking classes, demonstrations, tasting events and customized corporate programs under the guidance of professional chefs. By using simple, accessible, quality ingredients and learning about the culinary techniques needed to prepare them, clients learn to *understand* a recipe, not just follow one.

17 THIERRY MERET AND MARNIE FUDGE

French-born Thierry Meret trained at l'Ecole Hôtelière de Villebon in Paris, worked as a chef in Europe, and has led the kitchen at La Chaumière and La P'tite Table in Okotoks. A former culinary instructor at SAIT, the centre's chef de cuisine is inspired by regional cooking techniques and ingredients. Pastry Chef Marnie Fudge supplied restaurants with fresh herbs and award-winning retail culinary products before graduating from SAIT's Baking and Pastry Arts program. After completing an internship at Paris's Hôtel Lutetia, she returned to Calgary to work in the city's best hotels and restaurants while teaching at SAIT. Now she instructs classes and corporate groups and leads a yearly French culinary journey to the Périgord region.

downtownfood

This contemporary fusion bistro is located at the west end of Stephen Avenue. As the founder of the UrbanAg-Project, downtownfood has Calgary's first fully integrated rooftop ecosystem, including beehives from which the restaurant harvests honey and forty different types of vegetables, herbs and fruits. downtownfood makes everything in house and supports local, organic and small producers. The seasonal menu changes regularly to showcase ingredients at their peak.

18 DARREN MaCLEAN

Chef-owner Darren MacLean trained at Stratford Chefs School and Bijou restaurant. A strong proponent of the farm-to-table concept and especially local farmers, he pairs the freshest, most seasonal ingredients with Asian flavour profiles and techniques to serve up "true Canadian cuisine." A strong believer in sustainability, Darren is walking the talk with his rooftop eco-system, Ocean Wise seafood and house-made fare.

FARM Restaurant

Located on 16th Avenue SW, Janice Beaton Fine Cheese is Calgary's premier specialty retailer of artisanal cheeses, charcuterie, pâtés and accompaniments. The store also offers catering and cheese classes. In 2008, Janice Beaton opened FARM Restaurant, a casual tasting kitchen whose menu emphasizes simple, wholesome meals made with cheese, charcuterie and local products from farmers, growers and producers across the Prairies, all paired with the perfect drink.

19 JANICE BEATON

Janice Beaton grew up helping her grandmother tend the family's dairy cows on Cape Breton Island. A lifelong cheese lover, she opened Calgary's first specialty cheese shop in 2000, followed by FARM Restaurant nearly a decade later. In 2009, she was inducted into La Guilde Internationale des Fromagers for her work preserving the standards and quality of fine cheese. In 2014, Janice served on the jury at the inaugural Canadian Cheese Awards, which recognize outstanding cheese produced in Canada using the pure milk of Canadian cows, goats, sheep and water buffalo.

Il Sogno

Award-winning Il Sogno serves up contemporary Italian-influenced food in the historic, hundred-year-old DeWaal Block in Bridgeland. Fourteen-foot pressed-tin ceilings and original hardwood floors evoke an Old World feel in the heart of Calgary's "Little Italy." For over a decade Il Sogno has been lauded for its charming, comfortable and romantic dining room.

20 BRIAN DIAMOND

After completing his chef training at the Saskatchewan Technical School, Brian cooked in Saskatoon and Calgary before leaving to travel and work in Australia. Returning to Calgary, his enthusiasm and penchant for simple, elegant flavours made him a natural fit for Il Sogno's Italian-influenced cuisine, and he has been able to apply his philosophy that cooking should be fun with a light-hearted touch that allows flavours to shine through.

Jelly Modern Doughnuts

In April 2011, sisters and founders Rita and Rosanne Tripathy opened Jelly Modern Doughnuts in Calgary. It was the first gourmet doughnut store in Canada, an upscale artisan bakery offering more than twenty varieties of hand-made, fresh-daily, individually dipped and decorated treats made from local and organic ingredients. The ever-evolving menu includes tiny dough-nuts for cocktail parties and savoury doughnuts and "doughnut sandwiches." The concept has caught peoples' imagination, and Jelly Modern fare has been praised by Oprah and featured on *Hockey Night in Canada* and *You Gotta Eat Here*.

21 ROSANNE TRIPATHY
Co-founder Rosanne Tripathy received her first mixer in grade 5 along with various other kitchen tools. It was the perfect Christmas gift! A course on doughnut making at the American Institute of Baking gave Rosanne a solid foundation on which to launch Jelly Modern, and she has worked closely with pastry chef Grayson Sherman to learn about menu develop-ment, wedding presentations and special client events. In 2013 they won the Food Net-work's *Donut Showdown*.

Knifewear

Chef-owner Kevin Kent's fas-cination with Japanese knives began while he was working as sous-chef at Fergus Hen-derson's St. John restaurant in London, England. Upon his return to Canada, he became the chef at River Café in Calgary and started selling handcrafted Japanese knives out of a backpack on the back of his bicycle. Knifewear has since expanded to include five Canadian stores plus oc-casional pop-ups across the country. All of the stores offer classes in knife sharpening and cutting skills.

22 MIKE WRINCH
General Manager Mike Wrinch loves food, cooking, sunsets and sharp knives. A twentieth-century graduate of SAIT, he travelled to France and entered international cooking competitions in Paris. Returning to Calgary, he cooked professionally for fifteen years, including at River Café where he worked with and bought knives from Kevin Kent. Japanese cooking knives connect him to food and his love of preparing it.

Shown with Kevin Kent in photo

The Living Room

The Living Room is a timeless oasis of calm on 17th Avenue SW, an area known for great shopping, eating, drinking and people watching. The Living Room's spacious bar, groupings of couches, private dining room, soft ambient lighting and outdoor patio bookended with gas-burning fireplaces make it a popular spot for romantic dinners, a gathering of friends or lunch-time business meetings. The concept of shared, interactive cuisine for two or more brings people together.

23 KEVIN A. HILL
See Añejo.

MARKET

Entrepreneur and foodie Vanessa Salopek conceived MARKET as a restaurant committed to seasonal, local and sustainable produce and the principles of community. MARKET has built relation-ships with farmers, business-es and suppliers who practice ethical, mindful and responsi-ble stewardship so that diners know what they are eating, where it came from and how it found its way to the table. MARKET was voted a Top 35 People's Choice Award win-ner for Canada's Best New Restaurant 2013 as recorded by *enRoute* magazine.

24 DAVE BOHATI
Dave Bohati started his culi-nary career washing dishes in Victoria. He learned quickly from renowned chefs before moving to Calgary to work at Rush Restaurant, where he soon became the executive chef. Fortuitously, he kept crossing paths with Vanessa Salopek, who hired him to lead the team at MARKET. An award-winning chef, he competed in the Gold Medal Plates competition in 2013.

Meez Fast Home Cuisine

Meez is all about making healthy eating easy. Whether it's ready-to-heat home-cooked meals for busy families, special menus for weddings or other catered events or customized classes for home parties, every dish is made from scratch with minimal ingredients, maximum flavour and the highest-quality, locally grown meat and produce. Meez creates food that brings people together to share food and wine; it's like having your own personal chef on call.

25 JUDY WOOD

As a child, owner and Executive Chef Judy Wood helped prepare dinners when her parents were entertaining. She went on to earn her *grand diplôme* from L'École de Cuisine La Varenne in Paris, France, then began her career at Calgary's Four Seasons Hotel. She became the pastry chef at Toronto's David Wood Food Shop, then head chef at Buchanan's Chop House in Calgary before opening Meez. Twice a year she travels to France and Italy with small groups, touring and teaching the food and wine lifestyle she strives to live by.

Mercato

Mercato, or "market" in Italian, combines two family businesses: the Italian Center deli and meat market, founded in 1974 by Victor and Cathy Caracciolo, and Italian Gourmet Foods, founded in 1983 by their daughter Franca Bellusci and her husband, Peter. In 2005, son Dominic Caracciolo moved the businesses to the Mission neighbourhood where, under one roof, they grew into a 120-seat restaurant with an open kitchen. Mercato's simple, rustic, ingredient-driven Italian food emphasizes family-style dining and the flavours of southern Italy, where the family hails from.

26 SPENCER WHEATON

Victoria-born Executive Chef Spencer Wheaton was interested in food and cooking from a young age. He spent two years in southern France playing rugby and experiencing European food culture first hand, then moved to Calgary, attended SAIT and started at Mercato shortly after it opened. He has travelled extensively throughout Italy, gaining food experiences and techniques as inspiration for Mercato's menus. His highlight was foraging for porcini mushrooms in the mountains of Calabria, then preparing them on an open fire as part of a family feast held in the olive groves where Mercato's signature olive oil is produced.

Model Milk

A fun and sophisticated restaurant, Model Milk is located in a beautiful old building on 17th Avenue SW. A multi-level room with brick walls and hardwood floors has the overall feel of a studio loft, and the bistro-inspired menu is innovative, comforting and simple. Dishes are prepared from the best local and regional products the kitchen can afford, using them as simply as possible so that the flavours speak for themselves. And the main-floor bar is the perfect place to sip a carefully prepared cocktail or glass of wine.

27 JUSTIN LEBOE

Executive Chef Justin Leboe began his career washing dishes at Umberto's in Vancouver at age thirteen. He earned a degree in political science and philosophy then taught himself to cook. To gain experience he wrote letters to the best restaurants around the world and was invited to cook at Accolade in Toronto, Restaurant Daniel and Jean-Georges in New York, The French Laundry in Napa, The Peninsula Beverly Hills, and then at Waterloo House in Bermuda. After opening Rush in Calgary, he moved to Model Milk, which is an exciting departure from haute cuisine.

Muse Restaurant & Lounge

Voted one of Canada's Top 50 Best Restaurants for 2013, Muse is tucked into a cozy side street in Calgary's Kensington area. Its soft lighting, intimate seating and fine dining are perfect for a romantic evening or a casual, relaxing meal with family and friends. The menu features innovative Canadian cuisine made with seasonal, regional produce and served in multi-course meals with a complementary wine list.

28 JP PEDHIRNEY

Executive Chef JP Pedhirney earned his Red Seal certificate, then received further training at the Michelin-starred Blackbird Restaurant in Chicago. He has worked for some of Calgary's best restaurants, including River Café, CA Restaurant Group and Rouge Restaurant. Using the freshest seasonal, local ingredients and his experience, expertise and love of food, he creates carefully composed dishes and chef's tasting menus.

Native Tongues Taqueria

Native Tongues Taqueria, in the vibrant community of Victoria Park, serves classic Mexican street food in a soulful, electric environment. The menu ranges from classic tacos and ceviche to decadent torta sandwiches. Inspired by the success of the pop-up joint Taco or No Taco, Native Tongues joins the ranks of eclectic chef-driven restaurants currently shaking up Calgary's dining scene.

29 CODY WILLIS

A graduate of Stratford Chefs School and a certified sommelier, chef-owner Cody Willis explored a wide array of culinary styles at Open Bird, Model Milk and several pop-up events before finding his love for the rich flavours and simple ingredients in classic Mexican cooking. Having built a strong following for his nose-to-tail tacos made using modern techniques and paired with beer, bourbon, hip hop and wrestling, he was ready to open his own restaurant, and Native Tongues Taqueria was born.

Nicole Gourmet

Nicole Gourmet is a boutique catering company that focusses on personalized, custom cooking using the highest-quality local ingredients. From catering cocktail parties, dinner parties and corporate events to delivering homecooked meals and teaching classes, Nicole provides a wide array of services that allow Calgarians to entertain and eat well without worry. Her simple, sophisticated dishes are fun, interesting and comforting, right for any occasion and have found a steady following.

30 NICOLE GOMES

Trained at the Dubrulle French Culinary Academy in Vancouver, Nicole Gomes went on to work in France, Australia and Hong Kong before returning to Canada. She has cooked at many of the city's top restaurants, including Catch and Mercato, but her entrepreneurial spirit led her to create Nicole Gourmet. She was a contender on season 3 of Food Network's *Top Chef Canada*—and the last woman standing.

Ox and Angela Restaurant

Named one of Canada's "Best New Restaurants" by *Maclean's* in 2012, Ox and Angela, sister restaurant to UNA Pizza + Wine, is a popular Spanish tapas bar on 17th Avenue SW. The culinary traditions of Spain are given a subtle New World tweak, resulting in dishes that are familiar but fresh. A charming patio looks out onto the street, and there is seating in the lounge area, at the bar or in the restaurant proper. A large iron ox guards the door, ensuring that nothing tampers with Ox and Angela's magic.

31 STEPHEN SMEE

Owner and executive chef Stephen Smee was born and raised in Calgary. Self-taught, he began cooking at fourteen and has worked at The Inn on Lake Bonavista, Bonterra and Mercato with many talented chefs. His travels in Mediterranean countries influence his cuisine, create a strong foundation for his style and help keep the menus authentic and exciting. He lets the ingredients speak for themselves, believing food should be prepared and cooked quickly to capture the vitality of the dish.

Red Tree Catering

Red Tree Catering's menu follows the seasons, focussing on Asian and Mediterranean flavours in the spring and summer, followed by the full flavours of North Africa in the fall and winter. In addition to making food for individual parties and corporate events, Aaron Creurer, Susan Pataky and Melissa Bailot offer local, innovative take-out and delivery from their retail storefront in Calgary's pedestrian-friendly Marda Loop. The company is active in the community—judging at Gold Medal Plates, donating to the Banff Centre for Performing Arts and the Alberta Ballet and attending Wine Stage, a fundraiser for One Yellow Rabbit theatre group.

32 AARON CREURER

Founder Aaron Creurer is a long-time Calgarian who graduated from SAIT, started out with the Mescalero Group, ran a bakery and worked at Florentine Restaurant before launching Red Tree Catering with business partner Susan Pataky. He has travelled and cooked in Germany, Morocco and Thailand, and these cultures and flavours continue to influence his fresh, seasonal cuisine.

29

30

31

32

River Café

River Café, located at Prince's Island Park, was once a park concession stand. It was gradually transformed from a seasonal, open-air, full-service café to a gorgeous restaurant with a fieldstone fireplace, open kitchen, wood-fired oven and grill, and a bar made from an actual boat. Spacious yet cozy, River Café has spectacular views of the park, and the patio looks out onto the Bow River and the towers of downtown Calgary beyond. Award-winning River Café, and its new sibling, Boxwood, earned Canada's first LEAF certification for its sustainability initiatives, which include an edible garden, 100 per cent green energy power and a commitment to Ocean Wise seafood.

33 ANDREW WINFIELD

Award-winning chef Andrew Winfield, a graduate of SAIT, has a culinary style rooted in early farm-to-table cooking and emphasizes the purity of local, seasonal, fresh organic ingredients. In 2012, he was awarded the University of Guelph Good Food Innovation Award for his innovative use of Canadian ingredients.

Sidewalk Citizen Bakery

Started by Aviv Fried in 2010, the bakery specializes in sourdough breads and artisan pastries. The name and the food were inspired by Jane Jacobs's *The Death and Life of Great American Cities* and reflects the "sidewalk ballet" where people and business interact in a vibrant, connected space. Aviv uses flavours influenced by the Mediterranean and Levant regions combined with Canadian ingredients to make big, bright, sweet and savoury foods.

34 AVIV FRIED

After earning an honours degree in physics and a master's in biomedical engineering from the University of Calgary, Aviv turned down a finance job in Toronto to become an artisan baker. His quest to make the best bread has led him to train in Paris with sourdough master Jean-Luc Poujauran and in San Francisco with Chad Robertson from Tartine Bakery. Aviv's specialty is crafting and baking long-fermentation sourdough breads.

Sugo Caffè Italia

In 2001, Jesse Johnson and Angelo Contrada opened Sugo Caffè Italia in Inglewood, a neighbourhood that appeared to be on the cusp of change. Despite a bare-bones budget, they had planned a set price menu, but Sugo soon became one of the first restaurants in the city to offer a menu that changed daily, featuring dishes that were fresh, seasonal and affordable. Now renovated and expanded, the restaurant continues to highlight Italian dishes prepared with the freshest regional ingredients.

35 ANGELO CONTRADA

Co-owner and founding chef Angelo Contrada knew from the age of ten that he would be a cook. From his mother he learned the basic rule of good Italian cooking: keep the ingredients simple and the flavours will shine though. After stints in the top Italian restaurants in Calgary, he opened Sugo and created the caffè's signature dishes. Angelo has recently passed the reins in the kitchen to Joshua Stoddart, a graduate of SAIT who cut his teeth washing dishes and has worked in many of Calgary's Italian kitchens, including Capo and Il Sogno. He brings subtle changes to Sugo's classic dishes, keeping them authentic and delicious.

Shown with Josh Stoddart in photo

Teatro

Teatro, the long-standing sister to the newer Cucina Italian Market and Vendome Café, is located downtown in the historical 1911 neoclassical Dominion Bank building. Its high ceilings, Corinthian columns, nineteenth-century Parisian iron gates and hand-blown Italian glass create Old World opulence grounded by paintings from famous contemporary Canadian artists. Teatro's menu spotlights seasonal local produce and meats and house-made pastas prepared in a traditional Northern Italian style. Teatro boasts an impressive award-winning wine list.

36 JOHN MICHAEL MacNEIL

John Michael MacNeil grew up in New Waterford, Cape Breton, and graduated from the Culinary Institute of Canada on Prince Edward Island. Inspired by a video about chef Ferran Adrià, John started learning and integrating molecular and avant-garde cooking into his menus. He worked at Buffalo Mountain Lodge in Banff, then studied under Swiss chef and Michelin gourmand Urs Thommen as well as with Paul Bocuse. Back in Calgary, he worked with Dominique Moussu at Teatro before taking over as executive chef there and at Vendome Café.

UNA Pizza + Wine

UNA Pizza + Wine, sister restaurant to Ox and Angela, opened in January 2010 as a neighbourhood restaurant specializing in gourmet pizza with influences from California and the Mediterranean. Calgarians love a good pizza and glass of wine, and UNA's ambience, long bar, semi-open kitchen and use of social media and cell phones to update wait times for tables and call customers when their table is ready has made it an instant hit. Owners Stephen Smee, Jayme MacFayden and Kelly Black have enriched the Calgary restaurant scene, and pizza lovers thank them.

37 STEPHEN SMEE
See Ox and Angela.

Vendome Café

Vendome Café, the sister to Teatro and Cucina, opened on October 1, 2009, in the historic 1911 Vendome Block, which has housed the North Star Grocery, a candy store, a meat market and a café and children's store through the years. The brick exterior and charming hardwood-and-brick interior have an inviting Old World feel, and an affordable menu, bakery, fun drinks list and really excellent coffee keep drawing diners back. Vendome offers live music on Thursday nights.

38 ERIK BURLEY
Erik Burley, like most young chefs, started out washing dishes but moved up to line cooking and realized that he had an aptitude for the kitchen thing! He worked for the Delta Hotel in Fredericton, where he accomplished a three-year apprenticeship in just two years and won the provincial skills competition for New Brunswick. Following a move to Calgary and a cancer diagnosis, he re-evaluated his career and accepted the offer as Vendome Café's chef de cuisine. He places a premium on hospitality and treats customers as though they are guests in his home.

Yellow Door Bistro at Hotel Arts

Yellow Door Bistro's design is a marriage of classical and contemporary elements that work to create a comfortable room. Sister restaurant to Chef's Table, Yellow Door's bistro-inspired cuisine respects its history while embracing contemporary ideas and flavour profiles that keep diners fully engaged. Open for breakfast, lunch and dinner, the Yellow Door features a fresh cocktail and diverse wine list served from a temperature-controlled enomatic system that keeps wine fresh.

39 DUNCAN LY
Award-winning chef Duncan Ly represented Calgary at the Canadian Culinary Championships in 2014. He started his culinary career at the Wickaninnish Inn in Tofino and has worked at Diva at the Met in Vancouver, Calgary's Catch and the Elbow River Casino. He brings passion, energy and high standards to his position as executive chef of the Hotel Arts Group overseeing Yellow Door Bistro, Raw Bar and Chef's Table at Kensington Riverside Inn and the banquet operations of the Hotel Arts.

37

38

39

Index

Page numbers in *italics*
refer to photos.

with pâté di fegato (Tuscan chicken
   liver pâté), 108
   in pork braciole (stuffed pork rolls), 124
   in veal meatballs, 31
bread crumbs. *See* panko
breaded calamari, 37
brined pork belly, 21
brioche
   in baked French onion soup with braised
      oxtail, 158
   for Fried's eggplant sandwiches
      with soft-boiled egg and
      green tahini, 138
broth, lobster, 78–79
Brussels sprouts and
   chanterelles, 143
burnt shallot aioli, 98
burrata, radicchio salad with poached
   pears and, 84
butter
   almond butter, 23
   clarified butter, 26
   lovage butter, 136
butter lettuce, in Dungeness
   crab and grapefruit salad
   with coconut-lime
   dressing, 157
buttermilk
   in Mexican crema, 119
   in strawberry shortcake doughnuts, 89
butternut squash velouté, 154, 155

C

cabbage
   rhubarb-glazed weathervane scallops
      with braised bacon and cabbage,
      46–47
   in sesame slaw, 17
Caesar dressing, 151
Caesar salad, kale, 150, 151
cake doughnuts, 89
cakes
   flourless hazelnut cake with white
      chocolate sour cream ganache and
      raspberries, 34–36, 35
   goat's milk ricotta cheesecake with
      lemon and rosemary, 72, 73
   orange almond lavender torte, 32–33

calamari, crispy, with ancho chili mayo, 37
capers
   in beef tartare, 97
   on celeriac soup with pickled red
      onions, 118
   in Dover sole with sauce Grenobloise, 40
   in pâté di fegato (Tuscan chicken liver
      pâté), 108
   in vitello tonnato, 71
caramel cream, whipped, 90
caramelized onions and rice, 58
caramelized onions, in elk lasagna, 68
carbonara, wild boar, 29
carrots
   in braised lamb shanks, 54–55
   in dolsot bibimbap (mixed rice with
      vegetables), 14–15
   ginger and orange-glazed carrots, 54
   roasted carrot and split pea soup with
      Moorish spices, goat yogurt, toasted
      fennel oil and mint, 134, 135
   in sesame slaw, 17
CBLT (coconut bacon, lettuce and tomato)
   sandwich, 60, 61
celeriac
   celeriac soup with pickled
      red onions, 118
   in verjus-poached squid salad with
      radicchio and chili dressing, 132
ceviche
   seafood ceviche, 75–77, 76
   tuna and watermelon
      ceviche, 38, 39
chanterelle mushrooms
   braised rabbit legs with ricotta gnocchi,
      chanterelles and two mustards,
      26–28, 27
   Brussels sprouts and chanterelles, 143
   ricotta gnocchi with Brussels sprouts and
      chanterelles in a roasted garlic sauce,
      142–43
   in truffled mushroom
      risotto, 126
   in wild mushroom tart, 18
chantilly cream, 32
cheddar
   black truffle and white cheddar
      fondue, 95

cheddar and apple pie, 112, 113–14
   in Janice's bubbling mac 'n' cheese, 80
   in open-faced spicy tuna melts, 153
   in pastry dough, 113
   in stuffed chicken breast with
      pipérade sauce, 105–6
cheese
   burrata, radicchio salad with poached
      pears and, 84
   cheddar and apple pie, 112, 113–14
   cheddar fondue, black truffle and, 95
   cheddar, in Janice's bubbling mac 'n'
      cheese, 80
   cheddar, in open-faced spicy
      tuna melts, 153
   cheddar, in pastry dough, 113
   cheddar, in stuffed chicken breast with
      pipérade sauce, 105–6
   feta, for elote (Mexican grilled corn), 119
   goat cheese, cranberry mustard and
      fennel, steamed halibut en papillote
      with, 74
   goat cheese fritter salad with apples
      and toasted almonds, 82
   goat, in chorizo and frisée salad, 64
   goat, in warm golden beet and arugula
      salad, 20
   goat's milk ricotta cheesecake with
      lemon and rosemary, 72, 73
   Grana Padano, in wild boar carbonara, 29
   Gruyère, in baked French onion soup with
      braised oxtail, 158
   Gruyère, in Janice's bubbling
      mac 'n' cheese, 80
   Gruyère, in open-faced spicy tuna melts,
      153
   Gruyère soufflé, savoury leek and, 24–25
   mascarpone, in beef tenderloin
      and soft polenta, 148
   mascarpone, in garlic cream sauce, 87
   mascarpone, in leek and mushroom
      portafoglio, 86–87
   mascarpone, in tiramisù, 147
   mozzarella, on chorizo-mango-cilantro
      pizza, 140–41
   mozzarella, in elk lasagna, 68–69
   mozzarella, in pork braciole (stuffed
      pork rolls), 124

About the Authors

GAIL NORTON
(*left*) is at the heart of Calgary's food scene. As the owner of The Cookbook Co. Cooks and the publisher of *City Palate* magazine, she is passionate about sharing her love and knowledge of food with others.

KAREN RALPH
(*right*) is an avid cook and freelance writer. She works at Metrovino and writes extensively about food and wine.

Both Gail and Karen live in Calgary, Alberta.